CLASSIC SAFARI CAMPS *of* AFRICA

YAMAHA

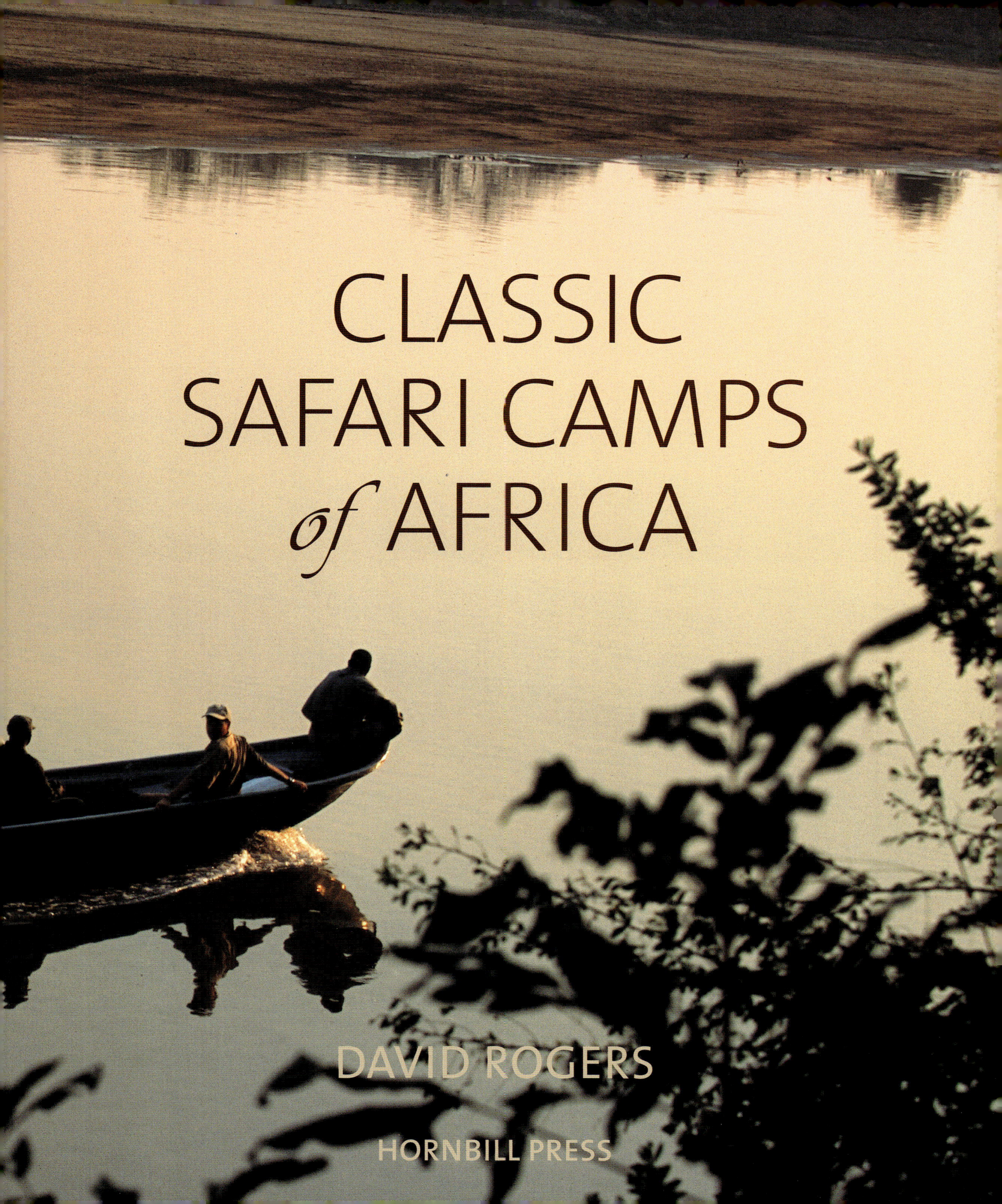

CLASSIC SAFARI CAMPS *of* AFRICA

DAVID ROGERS

HORNBILL PRESS

CONTENTS

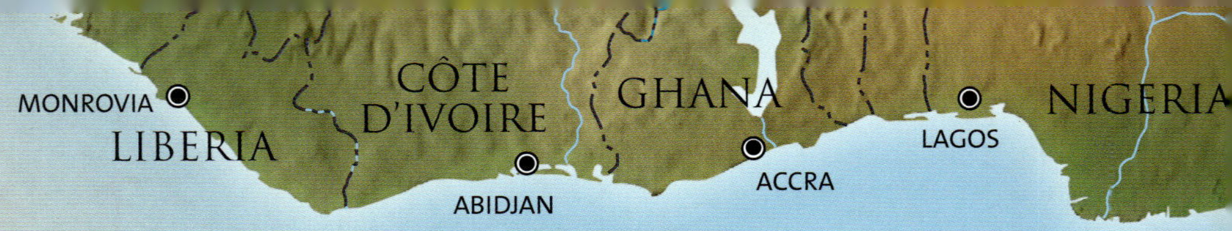

Classic Safari Camps of Africa

Mission Statement

Classic Safari Camps of Africa is an association of independent, privately owned camps and lodges in some of the most beautiful wildlife and wilderness areas in East and Southern Africa. Each of these unique establishments offers genuine hospitality and an intimate knowledge of Africa's natural environment, and is dedicated to conservation and the involvement of local communities sharing and conserving the spirit of Africa.

South Africa

1. **Ant's Private Bush Homes** — *Waterberg*
2. **Garonga Safari Camp** — *Makalali Conservancy*
3. **Jaci's Safari Lodge** — *Madikwe Game Reserve*

Namibia

4. **Wolwedans Collection** — *NamibRand Nature Reserve*
5. **Mowani Mountain Camp** — *Twyfelfontein, Damaraland*
6. **Onguma Safari Camps** — *Etosha National Park*

Botswana

7. **Selinda Camp** — *The Selinda Reserve*

Zimbabwe

8. **The Hide** — *Hwange National Park*
9. **Musango Safari Camp** — *Lake Kariba/Matusadona National Park*
10. **Nduna Safari Lodge** — *Malilangwe*

Zambia

11. **Tongabezi and Sindabezi** — *Victoria Falls*
12. **Chongwe River Camp** — *Lower Zambezi National Park*
13. **Robin Pope Safaris** — *South Luangwa*

Mozambique

14. **Benguerra Lodge** — *Bazaruto Archipelago*

Tanzania

15. **Greystoke Mahale** — *Mahale Mountains National Park*
16. **Sand Rivers Selous** — *Selous Game Reserve*

Kenya

17. **Tortilis Camp** — *Amboseli National Park*
18. **Elsa's Kopje** — *Meru National Park*
19. **Joy's Camp** — *Shaba National Reserve*
20. **Governors' Camps** — *Masai Mara*
21. **Loldia House** — *Lake Naivasha*
22. **Mfangano Island Camp** — *Lake Victoria*
23. **Cottars 1920s Safari Camp** — *Masai Mara*
24. **Loisaba Wilderness** — *Laikipia Plateau*

Uganda, Rwanda

25. **Semliki Safari Lodge** — *Semliki Wildlife Reserve*
26. **Apoka Safari Lodge** — *Kidepo Valley National Park*
27. **Sabyinyo Silverback Lodge** — *Volcanoes National Park*

CENTRAL AFRICAN REPUBLIC
CAMEROON
YAOUNDÉ
LIBREVILLE
CONGO
GABON
DEMOCRATIC REPUBLIC OF THE CONGO
Congo
Nile
ETHIOPIA
Lake Turkana
26 APOKA SAFARI LODGE
Lake Albert
KENYA
SEMLIKI SAFARI LODGE 25
UGANDA
KAMPALA
LOISABA WILDERNESS
LOLDIA HOUSE
JOY'S CAMP
19
MFANGANO ISLAND CAMP
22
21
24
18 ELSA'S KOPJE
SABYINYO SILVERBACK LODGE 27
20
GOVERNORS' CAMPS
23
NAIROBI
KIGALI
Lake Victoria
COTTARS 1920s CAMP
17 TORTILIS CAMP
RWANDA
Arusha
Kilimanjaro
Mombasa
BRAZZAVILLE
KINSHASA
TANZANIA
Lake Tanganyika
15 GREYSTOKE MAHALE
DODOMA
DAR ES SALAAM
SAND RIVERS SELOUS 16
Lake Rukwa
Rufiji
LUANDA
Lake Mweru
Lake Malawi
Luangwa
ANGOLA
ROBIN POPE SAFARIS 13
MALAWI
ZAMBIA
LILONGWE
CHONGWE RIVER CAMP
MOZAMBIQUE
LUSAKA
12
Zambezi
Cunene
TONGABEZI & SINDABEZI
11
MUSANGO SAFARI CAMP
9
Lake Kariba
HARARE
MADAGASCAR
Etosha Pan
6 ONGUMA SAFARI CAMPS
Victoria Falls
7
8
ZIMBABWE
Zambezi
Okavango Delta
SELINDA CAMP
Maun
THE HIDE
Bulawayo
5 MOWANI MOUNTAIN CAMP
NAMIBIA
Bazaruto Island
Benguerra Island
NDUNA SAFARI LODGE 10
Save
Mozambique Channel
14 BENGUERRA LODGE
Vilanculos
BOTSWANA
ANT'S PRIVATE BUSH HOMES
WINDHOEK
Kalahari Desert
TROPIC OF CAPRICORN
1
GABORONE
3
2 GARONGA SAFARI CAMP
JACI'S SAFARI LODGE
JOHANNESBURG
MAPUTO
Sun City
SWAZILAND
4 WOLWEDANS COLLECTION
Vaal
Orange
LESOTHO
N
W
E
S
CLASSIC SAFARI CAMPS OF AFRICA
ATLANTIC OCEAN
SOUTH AFRICA
INDIAN OCEAN
CAPE TOWN

Introduction

Classic Safari Camps of Africa is made up of some of the true characters of the African safari world. Many of them started out as guides taking small groups of guests into remote parts of Africa. They are extremely knowledgeable and are most at home when they are in the bush watching game or at the end of the day with a beer or a glass of wine watching the sun dipping over the horizon. These are people who are in the business because, for them, there is just no alternative to living in the bush and sharing it with other people. The camps that have been built reflect the individuality and style of each of the owners. When visiting the camps you feel as if you have discovered something of the spirit of the African safari. The standards and service are of a bygone era, with emphasis on guests' comfort, relaxation and enjoyment of an authentic African experience in the Classic tradition. In an increasingly corporate and globalised business environment, the authenticity and homely service that you find in these camps is refreshing.

Classic Safari Camps of Africa started in 1996 when a handful of property owners at ITB, a travel fair in Berlin, started throwing around the idea of creating an association of like-minded people who could use their combined talents and funds to market their properties at international trade fairs. Amongst that small party of original members (and they are still in the group today) was Aris Grammaticas of Governors' Camps and Jo Pope of Robin Pope Safaris.

Every year the members met at a different property, where the rules of the association were fine-tuned. Jo Pope recalls time spent at Little Governors', Wolwedans, Benguerra Lodge and Tortilis amongst others, where the group would go through the biz, brainstorm about the future and then play. 'We went ballooning over the Masai Mara, sat watching the amazing light on the Namib dunes and drank sundowners on a kopje together,' she says. 'The group was always around 30 people and you can imagine the evenings. I still remember Steve Edwards, dressed in his kikoyi, standing next to the fire on the beach at Benguerra telling us hilarious but very unrepeatable stories. And Stefano Cheli standing on the bar singing operatic songs. There was lots of laughter and fun.'

Not just any camp can join this elite group and whichever camp you decide to visit you can be sure that they share a similar ethos and standard. Potential new members must be inspected and voted for inclusion at the Classics AGM. They must have been in operation for a minimum of two years – except in the instance of an existing member opening a new camp – and all of the activities offered (including walking trails and safaris) must also be controlled or owned by the member. The camp must be owner-run or managed, or the owner must have an obvious direct, hands-on involvement, and the camps must be of a similar standard as well as being authentic. Finally, no Classics member should be affiliated to or have any association with hunting.

What a wonderful journey this has been researching Classics for this book. For a year, I have been extremely privileged to travel throughout Southern and East Africa, spending time in some of this continent's finest wildlife areas. I have sat beside gorillas, watched thousands of wildebeest cross crocodile-infested waters, drifted along great rivers and watched the seasons change in some of the great game parks of Africa. I have been in dry deserts, humid forests, misty mountains and on the great open plains. But apart from these incredible experiences, the book has also given

me the opportunity to make new friends in the Classics family and to reacquaint myself with others. I have also been deeply impressed by the very genuine dedication of these camps to their communities and also to their environments. The areas where they operate and the people and wildlife found therein would certainly be much the poorer if they were not in operation.

As I have visited – and in some cases revisited – each of the Classics camps, I have been entranced by the highly creative, extraordinarily likeable and interesting characters that run them. Each one of them has their own fascinating story to tell and I feel honoured to have been given the wonderful task of documenting these in this book. Please join me now on this fascinating journey as we travel from South Africa through Namibia to Botswana, Zimbabwe, Zambia, Mozambique, Tanzania, Kenya, Uganda and Rwanda, enjoying undreamed of hospitality in some of the finest and wildest parts of this great African continent.

DAVID ROGERS
January 2008

Ant's Private Bush Homes & Garonga Safari Camp & Jaci's Safari Lodge

SOUTH AFRICA

Ant's Private Bush Homes

Waterberg

SOUTH AFRICA

The Waterberg has inspired writers, poets and naturalists with its wide views. It is in this area that Ant's Private Bush Homes are situated. Ant's Hill (left and above left) has commanding views over the bushveld that surrounds the lodge, where sable and other game are found. The guests that come to Ant's enjoy an entirely flexible holiday with one option being picnic lunches (above right).

South Africa's malaria-free Waterberg has been the home of the Baber family since the 1800s. Ant and Tessa crossed paths in the mid-1990s and their relaxed style of hospitality has made Ant's Nest and Ant's Hill two very special destinations, for families, international horse-riders, honeymooners, romantic safaris, weddings, and even chart-topping pop stars.

'This is a bush home, not a typical lodge,' says Tessa. 'We aim to provide a flexible safari with plenty of activities, keeping everyone entertained from the youngest to the oldest, the fittest to the most in need of rest ... It's the Ant's way.'

The bush homes are situated on two reserves, which cover 4 500 and 5 000 hectares respectively, and the game that are found include rhino, buffalo, eland, zebra and sable as well as a wide variety of other species. They offer a range of activities from walks to big game viewing, and also horse-riding – but for many guests the real thrill of being here is to relax in their own private bush home.

Ant's Nest was the original home. It is situated in the folds of hills, with six sizable suites that overlook a heated swimming pool and a large lawn that spills into the bushveld where horses and wildlife graze together. One group usually books it in its entirety and it is easy to see why it is just the sort of place to take over with a family or group of friends.

Ant's Hill, a few hours' canter away, has a row of elegant and privately situated suites and living areas, all of which have been built to follow the contours of a precipitous cliff with spectacular views of the Waterberg Mountains. The bathrooms and verandas virtually melted into the bush – and a 30-metre waterfall that cascades right beside the lodge heightens the drama.

The homes are largely fashioned from natural stone, with arches and beams made of knotted wild olive tree trunks, and they are decorated with exquisitely carved old Indian chests, cabinets and day beds. Add copper taps, rugs, colourful kikoi cushions and riding paraphernalia into the mix and you have an idea of the original 'Ant's Style'.

There are two or three hosts at each of the lodges responsible for making sure that the guests are well looked after. They are all enthusiastic young people handpicked for their love of wildlife, horses and hospitality.

ANT'S NEST. The original home of the Baber family has been beautifully restored by Ant and Tessa and is nestled in the well-watered hills of the Waterberg Mountains. Each of the suites is as large as a small house, with a large bedroom, lounge and veranda for relaxing. The lodge has its own stables and guests can enjoy riding amongst some of the big game found here, which includes white rhino.

'Most of our guests stay for a week or more,' says Ryan Phelan at Ant's Hill. 'We start with handshakes and end with hugs and kisses. If they cry when they leave we know we have done our job.' The visitors' book, filled with drawings and pictures by guests, reflects this sentiment.

Guided walks, game drives, mountain biking and massages are on offer, but without a doubt the best way to get around the reserve is on horseback. More than 45 horses, ranging from Arab-Boerperd crosses to testy thoroughbreds, means everyone from children to riding professionals can find a steed. 'People with no riding experience come here, and after one ride they are hooked,' I'm told.

That got me going and, on my last morning, I pulled on a pair of chaps and threw my leg over a horse called Naivasha. We took a gentle walk along the rocky ridge above Ant's Hill and watched slivers of early light cut across the bushveld plains below. We walked amongst a herd of zebra. Their muscles twitched as they saw us, but then they continued grazing. Walking slowly back to camp I realised it was not only the mountain views from my private bush home that I would miss, but the people who had been my 'family' whilst I was staying there. Ryan, you certainly did your job.

The large gardens and inviting swimming pool make Ant's Nest a great place for families with children, whilst the candlelit boma dinners add to the romance of the African safari experience.

At Home in the 'Water' Mountains

Ant's Nest and Ant's Hill are part of an imaginative and successful conservation initiative called the Waterberg Nature Conservancy. Together with Marakele National Park, Welgevonden Game Reserve and other adjoining properties they create a wildlife playground of some 170 000 hectares, which is home to all of the Big Five and is gaining increasing recognition from UNESCO as a biosphere reserve.

The Waterberg – or literally, the water mountain – is laced by winding rivers that wend their way through ancient crumbling rocks, which are in places nearly three billion years old. There are several rock art sites and rock art smelting sites, which indicates that people have been living here for thousands of years. It was here that Eugene Marais, one of South Africa's greatest naturalists and authors, and one of the region's most famous children, gained his inspiration. 'We were living in a high, narrow valley,' he wrote. 'Plants grew and thrived wherever the smallest root-hold had been gained either in the soil or in the living rock.'

Thanks to conservation-minded individuals like Ant and Tessa, these kloofs, which lie only three hours north of Johannesburg, remain remarkably untouched. They have gained increasing popularity in recent years because of the wilderness atmosphere, the friendly and hands-on nature of its people, and the fact that it offers great game viewing in a malaria-free area.

Ant and Tessa, like many of the early pioneering adventurers, have a deep love and appreciation of the Waterberg. Ant, a bear of a man, is as at home in the saddle as he was in a rugby scrum and has kind eyes, a warm manner and, judging from his paintings, a strong artistic bent. Tessa came from Kenya where her family ran a beach hotel. After working as a tour operator in England she just happened to be hitch-hiking through the Waterberg and the rest, as they say, is history.

ANT'S HILL is high on a hilltop looking out over the bushveld and has a tumbling freshwater stream that runs alongside. The colourful rugs and kikois that decorate the spacious lodge interiors reflect Tessa's East African roots, whilst other subtle touches create a warm and welcoming atmosphere. Guests of all ages are made to feel at home.

The evenings are a special time in the Waterberg … And you can end a day at Ant's Hill in a variety of wonderful ways: reading a book on a comfy sofa, on a hilltop with a drink, or in your delightful sunken bath.

GARONGA SAFARI CAMP

Makalali Conservancy

SOUTH AFRICA

Garonga has a calm and very special atmosphere. You can feel it in the tranquil treetop seating areas and in the lavish tents. The originality is largely thanks to its colourful and warm owner Bernie Smith (in the game drive vehicle in a red shirt!) and, as you can see from the lions at the front gate, it all works naturally.

Bernie Smith came to Africa from England as a young man and fell in love with its wild places. He travelled extensively and started collecting the ideas that he would eventually bring to his own lodge. He set his heart on Makalali – a wild part of northern South Africa, west of the famous Kruger National Park – and in June 1997 he opened Garonga. Whilst Bernie admits that many of his ideas come from other countries, Garonga was the first in South Africa to offer massage treatments, include drinks in its rates and also not charge a singles supplement. It is also one of the best value lodges in South Africa, and Bernie, who lives at the lodge full time, is there to make sure that his guests get very special treatment and enjoy what he has dubbed his 'soul safari'.

Garonga is on stilts, with an indoor and outdoor dining area and a rim-flow swimming pool that melts into the bush beyond – and at night dozens of lamps and candles give it a warm orange glow. From the deck my eye was taken on a relaxing journey up a drainage line and into the deep bush with its fabulous trees.

There are just six tents, with white canvas draped over softly contoured, burnt orange walls, which gives them a traditional safari atmosphere with a generous touch of North African style. There is a Zen garden, too, and every day thoughtful

Garonga is all about romance … expect candle-lit dinners, decadent picnics in the upper branches of a jackalberry tree and stilted tents that invite quiet contemplation.

Dining at Garonga

Each month Bernie takes great pride in sending out recipes that have been tried and tested by his chefs to past and prospective guests. Here's one of the favourites:

FRENCH TOAST WITH CRISPY BACON
AND BRIE CHEESE DRIZZLED WITH HONEY

1 single serving

3 slices bread
2 large free-range eggs
Zest of lemon
Zest of orange
Oil for frying
3 rashers bacon
1 wedge Brie cheese
Honey

Cut out the centre of the bread with a round scone or biscuit cutter (optional). Beat the eggs lightly whilst adding the orange and lemon zest. Heat some oil in a saucepan and fry the bacon until crispy. Set aside. Heat some more oil and, when hot, dip the bread into the egg mix and fry off. When the bread is light golden brown in colour, remove from the pan and layer the egg bread, bacon and Brie cheese. Drizzle a drop of honey over the top for the final touch and enjoy!

notes such as 'relax' and 'enjoy' are raked in the sand. There are indoor and outdoor showers on offer, plus a hammock where you can lie and contemplate rattling francolins and lazily grazing impala. Elephant also seem to like Garonga – and lion too. A small pride hung around the waterhole and observed the gingerly approaching groups of giraffe and impala.

Little Garonga is even more intimate. The Hambleden, Chiltern and Buckingham Suites are fully *en suite*, with a central indoor and outdoor lounge. They have a private swimming pool, camp hosts and a chef.

Bernie has created a romantic atmosphere – and he does so in a decidedly English and gentlemanly manner. Sleep-outs are offered on a platform in a distant section of the reserve, where guests are left for the night, swathed in netting and on a most comfortable bed, to contemplate the wilderness.

The game drives at Garonga are wonderfully unhurried events. I also went on an educational walk, where we enjoyed the small things, such as spoor, beetles and seed pods. But if that is too slow for you there is the Exercise Walk. My favourite, though, was the solitude walk. 'Walk a good distance apart and don't say a word.' At the end we were to sit alone and meditate to the sounds of the bush. I looked up and watched a yellow-billed hornbill rise and dip lazily through the sky above – ahh, I thought, my soul safari is complete.

The lodge is in a dramatic bushveld setting, with tall trees that make your heart melt and a waterway that wends its way into the distance. If you are not sufficiently lulled by the calmness of the experience, then there are also massage treatments on offer.

The swing bridge leading to Jaci's Safari Lodge is 'guarded' by a pack of metal wild dogs. It takes you over the river and into the reception area where fun, originality and friendliness abound. This is what Jaci's is all about.

JACI'S SAFARI LODGE

Madikwe Game Reserve

SOUTH AFRICA

Since 1997 Jaci van Heteren and her husband, Jan, have lived in Madikwe Game Reserve on the edge of the Kalahari, raising their three children with elephant, lion and wild dog in their back yard, and at the same time creating a magical experience for their guests.

Jaci was born in Zimbabwe, where her family spent all their holidays in the bush, and Jan ran restaurants in Pretoria. So when they met, married and had children, the creation of Jaci's Lodges was a natural step for them both.

'We live the ultimate life,' says Jaci. 'We have no locks on the doors, no curtains – and when we can (weather permitting), it's just a short flight for us to get our children to school in Pretoria. Our lodges are a fusion of our own travel experiences,' she adds as she leads me into Jaci's Safari Lodge.

Staying at Jaci's Safari Lodge you feel part of the family – and the living areas ooze character. The diningroom is wide open to the kitchen and there is a circular open hearth that draws visitors together before game drives or for a friendly chat on chilly winter evenings. There are sofas on which to relax and read books and a winding staircase leading up to the bar.

'The trailing thatch is a throwback to our parents' holiday home in Mozambique,' she says, 'and the Wurlitzer jukebox is from our crazy

Coffee, hot chocolate and an open fireplace in the reception area at Jaci's Tree Lodge (above) await guests returning from an early morning game drive.

The Nare Suite (below centre) has its own pool, guide and chef.

The 75 000-hectare Madikwe Game Reserve, where the lodges are situated, is on the edge of the Kalahari. This biosphere supports bushveld as well as desert species, such as gemsbok and springbok. Its biggest success story, as well as challenge, has been reintroducing wild dog (right) to the reserve. It remains one of the best places in Africa to see these animals, the rarest of African predators.

restaurant days. The lodges are our home and they are furnished with things we find on our travels – I can spot a good buy doing 120 k's per hour and a typical journey will include several stops to make a new purchase or place an order for the curio shops.'

The eight 'tents', set in an established garden, have flaps to let in all the sounds of the bush whilst offering the solid luxury of a chalet. There is also the Nare Suite (once Jaci's family home), which is a self-contained bush home complete with private swimming pool.

Children are important at Jaci's and specially designed game drives are arranged with a guide who is trained to entertain and instruct youngsters. There is a special game-drive vehicle equipped with fold-up sides, seatbelts and a basket with hot chocolate and cookies. All the children get a special box to store their seed pods and other treasures, and a colourful 'ticklist' with some of the most common species found on the reserve.

Jaci's Tree Lodge, upstream from Jaci's Safari Lodge, is built on gently sloping ground overlooking the river. Jaci's Tree Lodge, which Jan designed, is built from rosewood and thatch. You arrive at ground level and are soon elevated on walkways amongst the leafy canopy of a tamboti forest.

The Jaci's Tree Lodge rooms are extra wide, with large fold-out doors that invite the forest into the room, king-sized double beds and oversized marble baths – a first choice for romantics. It is also decorated with Jaci's eclectic colours.

At Jaci's Lodges, they talk about the Top Ten, namely black and white rhino, buffalo, hippo, brown and spotted hyena, lion, elephant, giraffe,

JACI'S SAFARI LODGE (opposite top) is wonderfully original in its design, with bright colours and special touches, adding to the overall style. The 'tents' (top) are a mix of canvas and mortar, giving you the very best of both worlds. The river in front of the lodge attracts many animals and guests can often enjoy a spot of game viewing from their private decks or the privacy of the Nare Suite (above), which is situated over its own waterhole.

leopard, cheetah and, Jaci's personal favourite, the endangered wild dog. But the excitement of the bush is also about the small things such as dung beetles, chameleons and mongooses. It is also a malaria-free area and families are made especially welcome. On a special children's drive, I was nine all over again and made a toothbrush from a gwarrie bush, sipped hot chocolate on the airstrip, and won the contest to see who could spit antelope dung the furthest!

Both lodges reflect the personalities of Jaci and Jan; down-to-earth people who love nature, good food, good company and are full of fun. The staff, who become shareholders after five years' service, also nurture the spirit of hospitality that is Jaci's and it is not surprising that it draws many people, including myself, for second, third and fourth visits. Their warm hospitality, child-friendly policies and innovative designs and ways of doing things have also won them much acclaim. In 2004 and 2005 Jaci's Lodges were voted by guests to be the Best Game Lodge in South Africa. They were included in the *Tatler* Best Hotels in the World in 2005, and in 2006 were runners-up in *House and Leisure* and *Getaway* magazines. In 2007 readers of *Getaway* voted Jaci's Best Game Lodge in South Africa.

JACI'S TREE LODGE. **This entire lodge, including the dining area, outdoor boma, reading areas and bedrooms, has been built high in the canopy of the riverine forest.**

A TRUST IN PEOPLE

The friendliness and warm hospitality found at Jaci's is no accident. The company sources all their staff from neighbouring communities and involves them in decisions about running the lodge. They have also started the Jaci's Staff Trust, which is made up of 25.1% of shares in Jaci's Safari Lodge (Pty) Ltd.

'There can be no better shareholders in our company than the people who are actually looking after our guests,' say Jan and Jaci. 'We believe that this is a true empowerment opportunity for staff who stay with the company to become shareholders in the company that they helped to build.'

'The first five members were women and so are the majority of the 16 staff members who now make up the trust,' adds Jaci. 'Shows who has the staying power!'

'I am happy ... I don't know what to say. None of the other lodges have a staff trust ... only my darling Jaci and Jan. It means that I can work hard looking after Jaci's Lodge and have something in my account to look after me when I am too old to work any more.' AGGAI SEPHAI (RECENTLY A GRANDMOTHER)

'I am so proud to be part of the Staff Trust, as it shows we are good trustworthy people at Jaci's. We wish our best for this company that does us such a good thing to give us a Staff Trust. I am really happy as I am saving money for my children and my old age.' NAOMI MODISE (MOTHER)

'To me the Staff Trust means a serious commitment from the original shareholders to the people on the ground. It means that I, as a part owner, am now looking after my own and the reward is shared with me. But let me also say that I love the product, Jaci's. It is not difficult for me to be enthusiastic ...' PERRY DELL (MOTHER)

Wolwedans Collection & Mowani Mountain Camp
& Onguma Safari Camps

NAMIBIA

Wolwedans Collection

NamibRand Nature Reserve

NAMIBIA

Wolwedans is one of the largest private reserves in the world … a vast expanse of sand, mountains and blissful views that can be enjoyed at a number of wonderful camps, including Dune Camp (above left and opposite) and Boulders Camp (above right).

I walked alone from my tent one afternoon and was soon enveloped by the gentle curves of the dunes of the NamibRand Nature Reserve. It was so quiet that I could hear only my thoughts, but the desert was alive: a beetle scurried across the sand, birds circled overhead and far in the distance oryx stood motionless against red dunes. Everywhere blue skies, golden grass and red sands created a canvas of a thousand exquisite pictures.

NamibRand forms part of the Namib Desert and covers around 170 000 hectares, making it one of the largest private reserves in the world. Namibian businessman Albi Brückner, who established the reserve in the early 1990s, purchased 13 sheep farms over the next few years and removed all the fences, creating a seamless wilderness that today is 100 kilometres long and 30 kilometres wide. Albi's dream was to extend the desert wilderness of the adjoining Namib Naukluft National Park and create a place where wild animals could run free and where visitors could share in the beauty – forever.

The future of NamibRand is secured in a trust and the management of the park is handled by a team of experienced game wardens.

In 1993 Stephan Brückner, Albi's eldest son, created Wolwedans (the name of one of the farms), which today has four intimate camps that give visitors access to this amazing place.

'The whole reserve accommodates less than 80 visitors,' says Stephan. 'Our plan is that each person should always have more than 1 000 hectares to explore.'

Wolwedans has vast appeal to people looking for an authentic experience, without air-conditioning, spas or hairdryers. The rooms are made entirely from wood and canvas and are minimalist – and that's the way people love it. Guests stay a minimum of two days and often much longer. A man I met had booked in alone for seven days to experience the healing power of nature. Another guest burst into tears when she stepped into her room and looked at the view.

The early morning light plays across the gentle dunes of the Namib Desert at Dune Camp.

Investing in the Community

Stephan Brückner believes in investing in the Wolwedans staff, all of whom are Namibian citizens and many from the nearby Maltahöhe district. Some years ago Wolwedans started the Namibian Institute of Culinary Education (NICE) in Windhoek, which is a school and restaurant that plays an important role in providing skilled chefs to the Namibian tourism industry. More recently Wolwedans established the Desert Academy School (above), where 16 students a year are handpicked to take part in a training programme in housekeeping, waitering, administration, front office, kitchen and other housekeeping functions. 'It works very well,' says Stephan. 'We pay the students, enabling them to cover the tuition fees, and at the end of a nine-month cycle we get to choose the best of them to work in our lodges.'

Dune Camp has six tents built on stilts atop 250-metre-high grass-covered dunes. The views of mountains and sand are spectacular and so is the atmosphere. Whilst it is customary in many camps in Africa for dinner to be announced by the camp staff, hearing it in Nama in the charming wooden dining room is endearing. The local language is made up of a series of clicks, and because there are no words for chocolate mousse and other such luxuries guests are instead given such imaginative and roundabout descriptions as 'the dish is soft, tastes like sugar and is brown in colour'. The staff cannot help but guffaw at their own ingenuity.

Dune Camp (above) has glorious views and wonderful staff (left), who pose here before serving dinner. They announced the chocolate mousse dessert in the local Nama language ... an entire sentence of extraordinary 'clicks'.

The serenity and solitude of Private Camp (below and opposite) is unspeakably beautiful and a continuation of the desert landscape outside. The self-contained camp also features a romantic sala (opposite top) where you can stretch out in comfort amidst a sea of sand.

Private Camp is ideal for those wanting absolute privacy and solitude, and is a favourite choice of honeymooners and families with small children. This self-contained camp with two double rooms, a kitchen and dining area is an out-of-this-world experience, with a romantic sala where you lie in a large shaded bed surrounded by a sea of sand.

Dune Lodge enjoys a similar setting and atmosphere to Dune Camp, but instead of tents the stilted camp has wooden structures with roll-down blinds, a library, a diningroom, a swimming pool and a wine cellar. Mountain View Suite is a walk away with 200 square metres of decking and a large private lounge, bedroom and dining area.

The latest camp to be built – and by far the most sophisticated – is Boulders Camp. It lies in the south of the reserve against a tumbled backdrop of massive granite boulders, two hours' drive from the other camps, and is especially popular with international movie stars. It has five spacious tents and a central living and kitchen area overlooking a fertile valley where clans of San used to gather each year to hunt, feast, socialise and share ideas. Stephan has trodden as lightly as possible on this landscape, which has been proposed as a future National Heritage Site.

'We could dismantle all the camps in a few days,' he told me, 'and after the first rains there would be no sign that we were ever here.'

BOULDERS CAMP. The most recent addition to the Wolwedans Collection is in an exquisite region of the reserve and is built beneath a tumble of granite boulders that seem to have been placed here by some giant's hand. Guests stay for a minimum of three nights, enjoying game drives, walks and quiet contemplation in one of the most extraordinary settings in Africa.

Stephan Brückner (above right), behind the lens photographing Boulders, runs Wolwedans and is the son of Albi, who started the extraordinary reserve. When building here he was particularly careful to tread gently on a landscape where stunning *Commiphora* trees cling to the rocks. 'The San used to gather here for celebrations,' he told me.

Desert wonders

NamibRand is in the southern Namib Desert – a narrow arid strip along the west coast of Southern Africa that receives just under 100 millimetres of rainfall a year. It is the oldest and most species-rich desert in the world and the plants and animals that survive here depend almost entirely on the life-sustaining water of coastal fog that is carried inland on desert winds.

The views rival Sossusvlei (the very popular tourist destination about 80 kilometres to the north), but here at NamibRand visitors get to experience the sea of sand almost entirely alone. During the day it is also possible to go on guided nature drives over the vegetated dunes and past massive outcrops of granite. Oryx, ostrich, springbok, jackal and mongoose are readily seen and well adapted to survive in this arid landscape. Oryx, for example, have special chambers in their nostrils that help them to regulate their temperature, and they can survive almost entirely on the moisture obtained from eating plants. Even the gnarled, time-tortured plants have developed their own fascinating survival techniques.

There is also mystery here. Throughout the reserve are millions of bare, circular patches of earth, which are between two and three metres in diameter. These fairy circles, as they are called, occur from the Northern Cape in South Africa to southern Namibia and, although they are most probably caused by termite activity, nobody knows for sure. Interesting experiments have shown that plants will in fact grow in the soil, but only if it is removed from the site. At NamibRand there is a project whereby people can adopt a fairy circle and so make a donation to support desert ecology projects.

A lone oryx (above) stands sentinel on a dune at Wolwedans. The Namib is a wondrous place and the fairy circles (left) that dot the landscape enhance the magic of the forbidding terrain.

In the Namib Desert zebra, oryx, ostrich and other smaller creatures have devised fascinating ways in which to survive their harsh surroundings. Note the camouflage of this beetle (left) and the nutritious camelthorn seed pods (far left), which are a prized source of food for many animals.

Mowani Mountain Camp is the ultimate retreat, and a place of peace, tranquillity and solitude.

MOWANI MOUNTAIN CAMP

Twyfelfontein, Damaraland

NAMIBIA

At Mowani, architecture mimics nature in the most rounded way. The lodge has exquisite comforts and is a window onto a dry and forbidding landscape, where guests can set off each day in search of desert elephant as they follow the course of the sandy rivers.

Mowani takes its name from *M'Wane*, meaning 'Place of God' – and at dawn and dusk, when the crumbled and ancient granite rocks turn pink and long shadows outline the mountains, the incredible views of Namibia's dry and mountainous Damaraland landscape are heavenly indeed. Designed and built by André Louw (also co-owner of Onguma, see page 43), Mowani's unique domed dining and living areas echo the boulders between which it is built and there is a sense of living in a tastefully decorated African village.

The 12 luxury tents, all dwarfed by massive boulders, are built on stilts in East African style and each enjoys stupendous views. On a rocky outcrop nearby, with open-sided living spaces that fall away into the wide landscape beyond, is The Suite, one of the most spectacular spaces I have ever visited. It has romantic inside and outside bathrooms and comes with a butler who serves delicious meals on the private deck.

Mowani, in Damaraland's Twyfelfontein Conservancy between the Ugab and the Huab rivers, is a communal area where people and livestock live unfenced from free-ranging desert rhino and elephant, as they have for hundreds of years. I went on a game drive with Athan Gawiseb, who was born in this area, and it took under an hour to track down three large desert elephant. It is more difficult to track black rhino – the shy creatures tend to head into hard-to-reach places during the day. So, be prepared to wake up before sunrise and, if you find fresh spoor at a waterhole, to be on the trail for several hours. Whether you find them or not, the journey will be an adventure.

ONGUMA SAFARI CAMPS

Etosha National Park

NAMIBIA

DESERT FORTRESS. The Fort overlooks the vast emptiness of Etosha's Fisher's Pan, simply decorated with camelthorn trees and a variety of wild animals. The waterhole right in front of the lodge attracts animals throughout the day, including lion, zebra, oryx, wildebeest and giraffe.

Rising up from the wide plains of Namibia's Etosha National Park is Onguma Plains, The Fort, a lodge as dramatic as the landscape on which it stands. The lodge's 12-metre-high tower affords guests endless views across the bushveld and over the Etosha Pan. The Fort's design is a combination of Moroccan and other African influences and has thick, roughly plastered walls the colour of red sand and intricately carved African and Indian antique doors. Inside, away from the heat and dust, is a courtyard with trickling water and tastefully decorated areas with long billowing drapes that waft in the breeze.

'Who built this place?' – a question that I heard often repeated as guests escaped the heat into its cool and relaxing spaces. The answer is André Louw. Over the past 10 years he has masterminded a succession of stunning places, including Kulala Desert Lodge at Sossusvlei, Villa Verdi in Windhoek, Mowani in Damaraland (see page 41) and, more recently, the four lodges at Onguma. All fit boldly and beautifully into their surroundings, and yet each is designed and furnished in its unique individual style.

The Fort at Onguma opened its doors in August 2007, exactly 100 years after Etosha was

'Forts are synonymous with deserts,' says André Louw (opposite, bottom right). 'We obtained much of the inspiration from Morocco and combined it with some ideas of our own. The Fort needed to be in contrast with nature, and yet had to blend in at the same time … built for a few people in an oversized space … a place to live as kings and queens of your own castle.'

proclaimed as a game reserve. It is located on the 20 000-hectare Onguma Private Game Reserve adjoining the endless white plains of Etosha's Fisher's Pan.

The Fort has 12 generous Bush Suites, placed 50 metres apart for complete privacy. Each suite is designed as a mini-fort, with its own viewing tower from which you can enjoy a drink, finish your book or just simply gaze out across the plains. There are indoor and outdoor showers, luxurious fittings and wonderful views from a private deck. The suites have their own fireplaces for winter and specially designed, environmentally-friendly air-coolers for the summer.

Spend your days relaxing by the poolside or enjoying the tranquillity of the huge open spaces. Or explore the bush on one of the game-viewers and return to sundowners and exquisite sunsets, followed by dinner under the stars with wild animals at the lit waterhole as your companions.

When Onguma Luxury Safari Tented Camp opened in 2005 it, too, had critical acclaim from architectural magazines.

Each of the seven safari tents looks out onto an exquisite palm-fringed waterhole where many wild animals come to drink ... even the outside shower area has a view of the waterhole! There is also a swimming pool and tented lounge and dining areas.

TENTED CAMP. 'We chose browns, whites and greys for this camp, with a touch of green,' says André. 'All are colours of nature – you will find each one of them in a lion's mane or in an elephant's skin.'

Etosha National Park and its Surrounds

There are no fences around Onguma's camps – I saw lion from my bed at Tree Top, leopard from the dining area at Tented Camp and 12 giraffe from my room at The Fort. A stay here means guests have almost exclusive access to 20 000 hectares of bush where more than 30 species of mammal are found, including black rhino. The beauty of staying on a private concession means that you have the opportunity to go on night drives and on walking trails, which are privileges not allowed in most national parks.

Onguma's open vehicles also take daily game drives into Etosha and this is something that should not be missed. The 21 365 square kilometre park is one of the great game reserves of Africa. At its heart is the vast Etosha Pan, which is 130 kilometres long and 20 kilometres wide. The edge of the pan has natural seepage points that enable a variety of species to survive in the surrounding woodlands ... and here, in the cool shade of the trees, lion and cheetah await their prey.

Onguma Tree Top is the smallest and most intimate of the camps and is ideal for a small group of friends or family travelling together. This is where guests come to experience the bush in all its raw splendour. The camp fits in perfectly with the bush and with its rustic appeal of wood, canvas, sticks and grass is a great spot to sit back with a chilled drink and wait for the animals to come to you.

The four open-sided thatched rooms are comfortably equipped, with an outdoor shower and private viewing deck across the waterhole. All rooms are connected to the central dining area with wooden walkways. At sunset the drawbridge that links the camp to the wild is pulled up, and guests relax round the fire whilst the chef prepares a hearty African dinner over the open coals.

TREE TOP. All the rooms are built on stilts at tree level and overlook a reed-fringed waterhole where lion, giraffe, jackal and many antelope frequently visit.

Selinda Camp

BOTSWANA

SELINDA CAMP

The Selinda Reserve

BOTSWANA

Selinda Camp is situated on the Selinda Spillway – a miraculous region on the fringe of the Okavango where waters bring unparalleled life to the dry Kalahari. The camp echoes the textures of the environment and is decorated with fine furniture and with imagery taken by Beverly Joubert.

Northern Botswana is a miraculous place. The landscape here, which forms part of the Kalahari, is as flat as a giant plate and is so delicately tilted that it takes several months for the water to make its way from the highlands of Angola into the Okavango, the largest inland delta in the world. The floodwaters generally arrive during the dry winter months and when they do start to trickle slowly over the dry sands they provide an incredible web of life for myriad species, including birds, reptiles and mammals.

The Selinda Reserve, which is defined by the Selinda Spillway that links the Okavango Delta in the west to the Linyanti Swamps in the east, is a massive private concession covering around 135 000 hectares of this wilderness. It was here that *National Geographic* explorers-in-residence, Dereck and Beverly Joubert, made many of their documentaries and when the concession became available in 2005 they jumped at the chance to help secure its future from hunting and share it with other nature-loving people.

Selinda is exclusive, with four small camps (Selinda, Zibadianja, Motswiri and Walking Trails) accommodating a grand total of 28 visitors! This is a wilderness in the true sense of the word and, because the area is in a private concession, guests are able to enjoy the same wonderful

At sunset, guests head for a sundowner and often meet numbers of elephant with the same idea. The region is also known for its big cats and rare animals such as wild dog and sable. You seldom need to look far for stunning wildlife, including this exquisite painted reed frog (below).

game viewing as is found in Botswana's national parks, as well as other privileges such as walking, night drives and, where the landscape allows it, off-road driving.

Selinda is the flagship camp, with nine tents overlooking the spillway. Personally designed by Dereck and Beverly, it has the same sense of simple yet elegant artistry found in their documentaries and books. The design of the main areas incorporates the four elements of nature: touches of blue suggesting water; bleached wood and billowing white fabric representing the air; wholesome food and wine representing the earth tones; and finally fire, which is the fourth element – one is lit each night for guests to warm themselves at the end of the day.

The central area has 180-degree views over the golden plains and comfortable leather couches and sun-baked daybeds where you can immerse yourself in nature. In the evenings, dinner is served out on the star-deck beneath the southern skies.

You will feel that you are on a *National Geographic* shoot even whilst you are inside the lodge: above the wine cellar, which is guarded by two massive Zanzibar doors, is a room dedicated to fine art wildlife images taken by Beverly in this area. There are also individual pieces hanging above the beds in each of the nine luxury tents, which are beautifully furnished. The adjoining bathrooms have voluminous stone baths and hot showers.

Setting off each morning and afternoon down sandy tracks, beside lagoons and beneath towering palms, we panned the grasslands for signs of life. There are thousands of elephant in the area, which crowd the lagoons every afternoon. We also saw buffalo, giraffe, hippo, waterbuck, baboon and plenty of lion. The local prides have developed something of a reputation for targeting hippo, but the previous night a buffalo had been killed. We were drawn to the spot by the sight of dozens of vultures hanging off the thermals and found two lionesses and five cubs sleeping near the kill.

I took a few shots before it was time to return to camp and the comforts of a well-prepared four-course meal, a roaring fire and a bed draped with the finest percale linen. The sort of luxuries, I imagine, that Beverly and Dereck must have dreamed of when they were camped for so many years in a small tent on the bank of the Zibadianja Lagoon.

The most rustic option on offer is Selinda Walking Trails in the remote northern part of the reserve. It is open to a maximum of six guests at a time, who follow guides on foot for two or three days along time-worn elephant paths, returning each evening to their simply designed tented camp. Then there is Motswiri Camp in the extreme west of the reserve, a two-and-a-half hour drive or a short flight from Selinda Camp. It is the sort of place that appeals to purists like myself, with three Meru-style tents built on terra firma. Zibadianja Camp, on the banks of the Jouberts' favourite lagoon, has just three tents, all with their own private deck and telescope to sweep the plains.

'The wildlife is stunning,' says Dereck. 'Wild dog den here, lion chase hippo, and there are elephant everywhere. It is designed,' he adds, 'for people who want to stay for a month.'

The camp (top) is built on a small island in the middle of the flat Kalahari and as the waters rise each year the water slowly draws in on all sides. It is a place of extreme comfort, with lounging decks, tents with stunning bathrooms and wonderful views.

From early morning coffee with freshly baked muffins to dinner under the stars, your day will be filled with the wonders of the African bush. Early morning games drives are the best opportunity to see nocturnal species such as lion and leopard.

For the Good of Selinda

Selinda first became a tourism operation in 1995, but when it came up for sale in 2005, Dereck and Beverly Joubert seized the opportunity. They had been associated with Selinda for many years, having had a camp near the Zibadianja Lagoon until 1999. Avid conservationists, their concern over excess hunting on private concessions in Botswana was an added incentive to create a place where the wildlife could be assured of sanctuary.

They are both renowned *National Geographic* wildlife filmmakers, photographers, authors and conservationists, who have spent an enormous amount of time in the Selinda area over the past 25 years. Their films, including *Eye of the Leopard*, *Relentless Enemies*, *Eternal Enemies*, *Ultimate Enemies*, *Lions of Darkness* and *Wildlife Warriors*, have won numerous awards, including an Emmy. The Jouberts are Explorers-in-residence at *National Geographic* in Washington DC, although they still spend 10 months each year filming somewhere in the remote regions of Botswana.

The Selinda team now includes a group of friends, all of whom share their passion for this region. They are Colin Bell, founder of Wilderness Safaris, Mark Read, Chairman of the World Wildlife Fund in South Africa, Paul Harris, CEO of First Rand Bank, and Grant Nel, CEO of Selinda.

Not only have they ensured that no hunting will take place in this region for the foreseeable future, but they have also kept this special area open for photographic tourism. Furthermore, their efforts will continue to assist local communities with funding from the Selinda Foundation Trust, a fund that benefits conservation projects, schools and other projects for the well-being of the region's wildlife and people.

The Jouberts (above) are immensely talented and highly ethical conservation celebrities. These photographs (right and below) were taken by Beverly.

The Hide & Musango Safari Camp
& Nduna Safari Lodge

ZIMBABWE

THE HIDE

Hwange National Park
ZIMBABWE

The unforgettable sight of hundreds of thirsty elephant charging out of the trees towards a waterhole is regularly seen during the dry season in Zimbabwe's Hwange National Park. This enormous park, which covers 14 000 square kilometres (that's half the size of Belgium), is not only about elephant however: it has 108 species of mammals and more than 400 species of birds, making it one of the most diverse game viewing destinations in the world.

All Hwange's animals depend upon waterholes and at sunset hundreds of elephant (above left) may be seen on their thirsty approach. The Hide is a wonderful base to explore this great reserve and the sumptuous bush breakfasts (above right) are a treat.

The Hide, which is located in the western area of the park, was started by Zimbabwean Tom Preston, who leased the land from the National Railways of Zimbabwe in 1992. It has been going strongly ever since and has been voted best tented safari camp in Zimbabwe nine times. Tom passed away in 1995, shortly after The Hide won its first award, and since then much of the responsibility has been taken on by his family.

Tom's wife, Lorraine, told me how much he loved the bush and the industry and his memory is everywhere: he built the double-storey A-framed main area, the 10 rooms with their authentic donkey boilers and the waterhole where elephant regularly come to drink. There are also two hides; one is made from an old container that Tom sank deep into the ground right on the water's edge.

The Hide is clearly popular. There was not an empty seat at the sturdy 24-seater diningroom table that dominates the main complex. For many of the guests, who were welcomed at dinner, this was their fifth or sixth visit. Most of the staff had worked here upwards of six years and in many ways it was like a family gathering.

The bath in the Honeymoon Suite is open to nature and is
a fantastic spot to soak and watch the sunset.

The Hide overlooks a pan where elephant and buffalo frequently come to drink. Two hides are built here, and the photograph above gives a good idea of the amazing perspective. To get even closer to nature, guided walks (right) are a great way to see the park.

The Animal Planet television channel had recently been in camp to film *Big Five Challenge*, where contestants have to use their wits to track down lion, leopard, rhino, elephant and buffalo. The arrival of Rovos Rail, a luxury steam train that stops at the nearby Kennedy Annex on its way from Bulawayo to Victoria Falls to give its visitors a taste of Hwange, was also a hot topic.

Then, of course, there was the usual talk of the day. Hwange fails to disappoint and guests were thrilled about sightings of a pride of lion, a herd of 50 sable and more than 200 elephant at the two nearest waterholes (Kennedy One and Two) .

'So what about tomorrow?' guests were asked over coffee. 'A walk through the park?' Walking through Hwange in the company of an armed professional guide is a thrilling experience. Some of the guests could not wait for tomorrow and opted for a night drive.

I slipped away for an early night in my luxurious safari tent. Wood smoke filtered up from the donkey boilers and from my veranda I could see the shapes of 20 elephant drinking at the waterhole.

LEGENDS OF HWANGE

'The true legend of Hwange,' Lorraine Preston says, 'was Ted Davison. He was the first warden of the park and he built it from scratch.' In Ted Davison's own book on Hwange, Tom Bulpin recalls in the prelude how the young Ted embarked on the massive task when he was 'twenty-two years old, single, and the budget for his first year's work (salary and all expenses) was 500 pounds'.

The historical picture above of Ted was taken at Guvalala Waterhole. 'My dad hated having his photo taken so we have very few posed pics of him facing the camera!' wrote his son John Davison. 'His beloved elephant were always far more important to him than publicity for himself!'

Modesty runs deep in Hwange, for the staff at The Hide must also take much credit for keeping this wonderful park on its feet. They support Friends of Hwange Trust, which maintains 10 waterholes across the park, supplying fuel and maintaining pumps. 'We can't just run two waterholes (Kennedy One and Two) because hundreds of elephant would concentrate on them and that would be detrimental to the vegetation,' says Angus Preston. The Hide also works closely with the Zimbabwe National Parks and Wildlife Authority offering logistical support building roads.

The Hide Family, who have played a major role in the conservation of Hwange, include (from left) Bridget Wolhuter, Barry Wolhuter, Angus Preston, Lorraine Preston and Lauren Gouma.

MUSANGO SAFARI CAMP

At sunset, staff at Musango set up hurricane lamps along the pathways to guide guests to their rooms.
In the early mornings these forests echo with the sound of birdsong.

Lake Kariba/Matusadona National Park

ZIMBABWE

The swimming pool (above) and all of the rooms (below left) overlook the lake.

Canoeing (below centre) along the shoreline of the Matusadona National Park and within the Musango private concession and Nyamasango Creek, can be an exhilarating experience.

Steve Edwards (below right) shows off some of the fossils he has collected over the years.

Sunset over the vast expanse of Kariba is such a deep shade of orange and red that it creates the most spectacular vistas I have ever seen. And with an elephant or a few dead trees to create silhouettes in the foreground it has all the ingredients for award-winning and unforgettable photographs. This vast man-made lake covers 5 180 square kilometres (the size of Wales) on the Zambezi River – one of Africa's greatest waterways – and the tiger fishing and large concentrations of big game make for an irresistible wilderness experience.

Steve Edwards worked for the Department of National Parks and Wildlife Management for 18 years (four as warden of Matusadona National Park). When he retired in 1990 he followed his dream by setting up Musango Safari Camp on a Kariba island, next to game-rich Matusadona.

The tented rooms are in thick forest and all face east over the lake, towards the rising sun. A bright green grass called *Panicum repens* covers the shoreline here and provides grazing to a vast array of wildlife, especially large herds of elephant and buffalo. The public areas are on the narrowest part of the island so that you can catch the sun as it rises and sets from the same poolside spot!

Steve is a wonderful safari companion. He has a dry sense of humour, a deep knowledge of the bush and a quiet demeanour that leaves you feeling safe even when you are walking with lion, buffalo or rhino. And you may very well find yourself in this situation! With the exception of giraffe and wildebeest, the region has just about every species of animal found in Southern Africa.

During Operation Noah in the 1960s most of the animals were relocated to this area and it

OPERATION NOAH

Lake Kariba is about 240 kilometres long and more than 100 metres deep. The shores are shallow, however, and are fringed by the fingers of the dead hardwood trees that once grew in this valley.

When the Kariba wall was completed in 1959 and the level of the lake began to rise, thousands of animals were in danger of drowning. When senior ranger Rupert Fothergill, Frank Junor (a young scientist) and Brian Hughes arrived it was the start of Operation Noah. Over the next two years, and with additional funding and assistance, they moved more than 5 000 animals, including 50 black rhino (below), to the mainland, particularly the Matusadona National Park. It was the largest animal relocation programme in history and many darting and capture techniques were pioneered.

In addition to jellyfish, shrimp, mussel and terrapin, the lake is also home to 42 species of fish, including nkupe, chessa, bottlenose, vundu, barbel, bream and tiger fish. At night the waters are bejewelled by fishing boats catching kapenta, a freshwater sardine introduced from Lake Tanganyika and now a major industry.

Lake Kariba supports many species of fish, but it is the tiger fish (above) that provides the best sport. All fishing here is catch and release.

has one of the highest concentrations of buffalo, lion and black rhino anywhere in Africa. Tracking black rhino on foot is a thrilling experience ... and guests usually get great views of them. More leisurely morning walks, scenic canoe trips and bird-watching are also offered on the fertile green plains and river system at the back of the camp. A remarkable 480 bird species occur, and these include specials such as narina trogon, Lilian's lovebird, Böhm's spinetail, white-backed night heron and Pel's fishing owl.

Sitting in the camp one summer afternoon, Steve brought out a collection of fossils that date back to the Triassic, more than 150 million years ago, as well as some prehistoric lung fish tooth plates dating from the Devonian period that are amongst the oldest fossils in Southern Africa.

The indigenous Batonga people were largely displaced by the construction of the lake but still live along its shores where they support their families by fishing. I went on a fascinating visit to the village with Elijah Garisamoyo, who has worked for Steve since the start of the camp and is now an accomplished guide. He told me that many of his family live across the lake in Zambia and to see them he has to embark upon a two-day journey.

Some of the older villagers still believe that the river spirit Nyaminyami was greatly displeased by the building of the dam. They say he was philandering downstream when the dam wall was built; he is now very lonely and only the dam's destruction will reunite him with his wife.

During summer the striped and impressively toothed tiger fish are at their most active and they offer excellent sport. It is pretty common to pull in what Steve calls 'rats and mice' from the shores here, but there are also plenty of big five-kilogram tigers to keep fishermen on their toes. We also went boating towards Matusadona, where elephant and buffalo patrol the grass-covered plains. Hippo raised their heads here and there and giant crocodile slid into the water. At Starvation Island orphaned wild dog are held by the Zimbabwe Department of National Parks before reintroduction to the mainland. Imagine our delight when we spotted them from the boat as they bounded after a herd of impala.

The bar and dining area (top) adjacent to the swimming pool, where staff are always smiling and ready with a cold refreshment. Starvation Island is just a short boat ride from the lodge and is the best spot to find wild dog (above). An aerial view of Musango (above right), which is along the narrowest part of the peninsula. Canoeing and guided walks take place in the backwaters behind the lodge.

Nduna Safari Lodge

Malilangwe
ZIMBABWE

Nduna, which is on the shores of a dam where hippo, crocodile and fish eagle are regularly seen, is in the 50 000 hectare Malilangwe reserve adjacent to Gonarezhou National Park. Malilangwe has one of the largest rhino populations in Southern Africa and spectacular sandstone cliffs.

Large herds of elephant, buffalo, antelope and other game seemed to be around every corner at Malilangwe – and just when we were ready to return to the lodge after one of the most wonderful game drives I can remember we came across two young lion grappling with a fully grown buffalo. Also catching the action was Emmy Award-winning documentary film-maker Kim Wolhuter, who has worked all over Southern Africa and has made Malilangwe his home. 'This is the most extraordinary place I have experienced,' he told me. 'I could stay forever.'

Malilangwe, meaning 'call of the leopard' in Shangaan, covers an enormous 45 000 hectares in Zimbabwe's South Eastern Lowveld and shares a 17-kilometre-long border with Zimbabwe's Gonarezhou National Park. Despite being the same size as the entire Sabi Sands in South Africa, what makes Malilangwe even more special is that there are just two lodges (Nduna and Pamushana), both of which cater for only a handful of guests.

Zimbabwean Ray Sparrow was the original landowner here and still lives on the property. He was dressed in a safari suit with cane and pith helmet and still looked every bit the part of the colonial explorer. 'I came here in 1948 as a cattle rancher,' he said. 'We soon found out these hills were a den for lion. There was no value in wildlife in those days and we could not tolerate them.'

This view changed, however, and in 1972 Ray developed a primitive tented camp at the foot of a ring of towering sandstone hills, which he called Lonestar. In the 1990s this became Nduna, a traditional safari lodge with six comfortable rooms, all of which overlook a sprawling dam. It gets hot here in summer, but the rooms are air-conditioned and there is a pool for cooling off. Lunches are served beneath the canopy of mountain acacia

trees overlooking the lake with its hippo, crocodile and abundant bird life. There is a boat moored beside the lake for sundowners and fishing.

Malilangwe's greatest attraction is the game – and it is exceptional. The Big Five are all found here and rhino are in especially large numbers (there are 56 black and 75 white rhino). These rare pachyderms can be tracked by vehicle and on foot. Exploring the reserve is an amazing experience. It has 38 habitats, including riverine forests, miombo-covered sandstone hills, acacia thicket and mature cathedral mopane woodlands, which support an extraordinary diversity of antelope – sable, roan, eland and smaller species such as klipspringer, oribi, grey duiker, steenbok, grysbok and Livingstone's suni can be found here. Amongst an impressive 500 bird species are 17 diurnal raptors, which include the magnificent Verreaux's eagle, African fish eagle, crowned eagle, tawny eagle, bateleur, marshall and African hawk eagle, as well as 11 different species of owl.

For thousands of years the San made their homes in the game-rich Malilangwe Hills and there are over 120 rock art sites with exquisite murals depicting wild dog, giraffe and many other species. I could almost picture these diminutive hunter-gatherers painting with blood and other natural pigments and using rudimentary brushes made from eland hair.

It is rare to find a place with such diverse attraction and also such heart. The work that is being undertaken with the neighbouring community is exemplary (see the box) and considerable scientific research is being supported.

'Malilangwe is not just about seeing game,' says Jason Turner, who is the tourism manager. 'Guests are making a significant contribution to the conservation and community development of the area.'

The lounge at the lodge (above) is typically decorated in African style and a selection of reading material is available to guests who wish to while away the afternoon. Days at Nduna can become very hot during the summer months, but the bedrooms are air-conditioned and guests can also cool off in the swimming pool.

The Malilangwe Trust

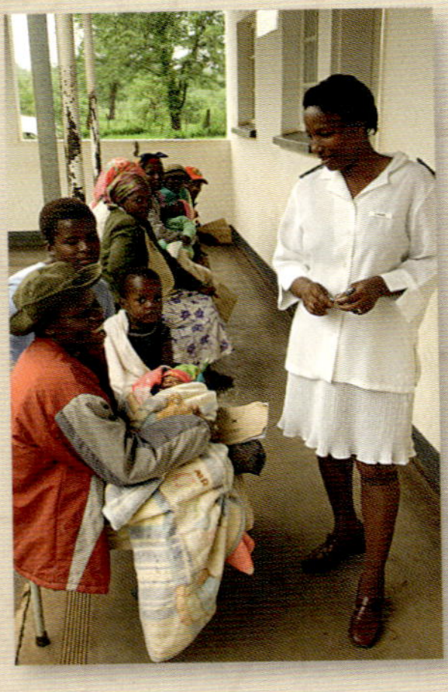

The Malilangwe Trust was formed in 1994 and employs 283 people on a permanent basis to run its lodges, anti-poaching and other estate initiatives and activities. The primary focus of this non-profit organisation is sustainable conservation and neighbour and community outreach programmes, whereby funds are generated through commercial tourism. The Trust has had minimal incidence of poaching in recent years and this is largely a result of overwhelming community support for Malilangwe.

I went to the clinic, which was set up by the Trust, to find out more about their Neighbourhood Outreach Program. 'There was so much poverty in this region before Malilangwe,' Sister Sithole told me.

The Trust has 506 different feeding stations and provides 25 000 children under the age of five with a daily meal. An estimated 23 million meals have been served in the four years that the feeding scheme has been in operation. The Trust has also set up small-scale irrigation projects to help communities to grow their own food. An estimated 250 000 people a year are touched in some way by the Trust, with the furthest afield being more than 100 kilometres away.

'Malilangwe really has the community at heart,' says Sister Sithole.

There are many rock art sites (above) in the reserve dating back thousands of years. This area was also along a trade route leading to and from Great Zimbabwe and there are remains of Iron Age settlements from this period.

It took this young male lion and his brother nearly 24 hours to subdue this large buffalo (below). The reserve is not just about the Big Five, however, and the diversity of plants (above) reflects 38 different habitats.

Tongabezi and Sindabezi & Chongwe River Camp & Robin Pope Safaris

ZAMBIA

Romance at its best at Tongabezi, as the last rays of the sun disappear over the horizon and the lantern light of the San Pan reflects off the still surface of the Zambezi.

TONGABEZI AND SINDABEZI

Victoria Falls
ZAMBIA

Tongabezi's suites (above left) have wide views onto the river and recall a bygone and romantic era. A guest kicks back on Sindabezi Island (above right) with a gin and tonic and a view of the Zambezi River.

Sitting at a table set with fine white linen, on a floating pontoon (called a San Pan) in the middle of the Zambezi, enjoying fine red wine and the company of lodge owner Ben Parker and his wife, Vanessa, is a quintessential Tongabezi moment. Just as we were discussing the time when Ben and I flew the length of the Zambezi in his microlight, a gentle thud against the side of our pontoon announced the arrival of our meal. Two Zambian waiters were holding trays aloft whilst the third was doing his best to steady the canoe in the swiftly flowing Zambezi current. And, if that was not enough, then came the choir. They too arrived in a canoe to wish me well and welcome me to their lodge.

There is something refreshingly different about Tongabezi, and every time I go there it has a new discovery to be had. It is a lodge with adventure in its heart and was started in 1990 by English adventuring friends Ben Parker and the late Will Ruck-Keene. They built 24 kilometres upstream from Victoria Falls at a time when there were very few lodges on the Zambian side of the river. It was so original that it immediately made headlines in travel magazines across the world. 'The honeymoon suite is worth getting married for,' wrote the *New York Times* travel editor.

Over the years I have spent glorious times at Tongabezi, sleeping in riverside rooms such as the Bird House, the Dog House, the Tree House and the Honeymoon House, calling for my tea or coffee using the antiquated wind-up telephones that are one of the curious features that make this lodge so unusual.

A Playground for Adventure

Ben Parker (left) flies microlights, a single-engine plane, goes to work in a canoe, and is in his element paddling alone along a deserted stretch of the Zambezi. The town of Livingstone is about adventure and has a menu of white-knuckle activities on offer. The stretch of water below the falls is the most exciting one-day commercial whitewater rafting in the world, with a host of rapids such as the Overland Truck Eater to prove their point. You can also leap off Victoria Falls Bridge with a bungy-cord round your ankle, dangle precariously above the raging river, go riding on an elephant, or simply take a canoe ride along the river and see elephant coming down to drink.

If you think that 'Tea on Livingstone Island' sounds like a gentlemanly affair, you would be right, but it is also pure Tongabezi adventure. We walked hand-in-hand along the slippery lip of the falls, through the swirling clouds of mist, and stood at the very spot where David Livingstone had his first view of it more than 150 years ago. It is even more exciting during the dry season, when it is possible to swim in a pool centimetres away from the yawning 100-metre drop.

Victoria Falls and the area surrounding it is a lure for adrenalin junkies and visitors can participate in a number of extreme sports, such as bungy-jumping, whitewater rafting or canoeing up the Zambezi.

TONGABEZI. **Bird House (above) has sweeping views across the Zambezi, a sunken open-air bath and its own valet. After breakfast on the deck (right) guests head off for adventures such as canoeing (below) or lunch at Livingstone Island on the edge of the falls.**

The Tongabezi Trust School

Vanessa Parker and the teachers and students of the Tongabezi Trust School. From its humble beginnings in 1996 as a preschool with only 15 pupils, the school has grown over the years and is now a primary school with over 100 students.

Tujatane – a trust school started by Vanessa Parker in May 1996 – is one of the most heart-warming success stories to have come from Tongabezi. Vanessa originally came to Livingstone as a volunteer teacher and, after marrying Ben, started a school in a single room just behind the lodge for the staff's children. Visitors to Tongabezi were so impressed that donations started to flow and thanks to them the school now has five classrooms, a computer room, a library, an amphitheatre for the arts, and it caters for over 100 children. It is an impressive school in an area where educational facilities are in very short supply and has drawn many children from surrounding communities.

'Some of them are from very poor homes,' says Vanessa. 'Thanks to Unicef, we are able to give them a meal at the start of each day.'

The school concentrates heavily on the arts and their dramatic productions and poetry readings have won them many awards and much acclaim – even from the Zambian president.

There is also plenty for birders, including these white-fronted bee-eaters (above), seen on an island in the river.

The Dog House (right) is right on the water's edge ... a king-sized bed, luxurious linen and airy mosquito netting assure a great night's rest.

More adventure and romance can be had at Sindabezi Island. This intimate, five-roomed sister lodge lies a 20-minute boat ride away on a remote island right in the middle of the river. Sitting on my deck with the sun setting between my feet and a hurricane lamp hanging from a nearby tree, I could have been the only person in Africa.

Ben and Vanessa have a wonderful home on the banks of the river called Tangala House – and they move out (increasingly regularly!) to make way for family groups and guests who come to share their private, dream-like view over the Zambezi.

SINDABEZI. This intimate lodge, which has just five rooms, is on an island in the middle of the Zambezi and is often occupied by small groups and families. The open-fronted chalets and private decks mean guests can get up close with nature.

CHONGWE RIVER CAMP

The Albida Suite overlooks the confluence of the Zambezi and Chongwe rivers. This private camp has its own guides and dining area and is furnished with a combination of period furniture, soft cream sofas and richly woven carpets.

Lower Zambezi National Park

ZAMBIA

Canoeists set off for an adventure from Chongwe River Camp (above) along the shores of the Lower Zambezi National Park. Whether you stay at the rustic Bushbuck (below left), Albida (below centre) or River Camp (below right), there is always the heart-stopping thrill of having elephants right in camp.

Chongwe River Camp is spectacularly situated on the boundary of the Lower Zambezi National Park, at the confluence of the Chongwe and Zambezi rivers, with stunning views of the Escarpment and across the Zambezi River towards Mana Pools. Downstream from Kariba, it is here that the river enters a wide and spectacular valley where forests rise up to a densely vegetated escarpment.

Christiaan Liebenberg came here in the early 1990s and established a small camping site at the confluence of the Chongwe River. It was a prime site – one that had been used centuries before by explorer David Livingstone whilst navigating a route up the Zambezi, and also by the hunter Courtney Selous. This is a premier wildlife region with a diverse selection of mammals and a wide variety of birds to be seen. With Christiaan and his father as hosts, Chongwe River Camp quickly established itself as a regular stop-off for canoe trails in Zambia.

'Zambia has always been well known for simple camps in remote areas,' Chris told me. 'As things are upgraded we try to stick to what Zambia is known for. That is smaller, rustic camps with open-air charm and only the indispensable luxuries.'

Chongwe River Camp retains the atmosphere of an adventurer's camp, where the beer is cold, the fire is hot and the people are friendly. It is still family run and some of the staff are Chris's university friends. The camp has eight tents with patios and charming open-air bathrooms at the back. They are beneath a grove of albida trees in a landscaped garden that has neat paths, a swimming pool, and a dining area right on the river.

Adjacent to Chongwe River Camp, but totally private in its own camp and with its own guides, is the Albida Suite. It has two octagonal tented rooms, a grand dining area decorated with fine period furniture, cream sofas, and richly woven carpets, and is situated right on the river. The ferro-concrete walls and canvas are the New Age colonial stamp of the acclaimed architect Neil Rocher and, despite its sophistication, it is still open to the elements in true Zambian style.

Rocher also designed Chongwe House – situated midway between Chongwe River Camp and Bushbuck – which is a joint venture with Jo Pope of Robin Pope Safaris. This masterpiece took a year to build and has a deck, riverside pool, furniture created out of fallen logs, and its own chef and hosts.

The simplest of the accommodation options is Bushbuck. 'More and more people are steering away from luxury and are looking for a traditional wilderness experience,' Chris told me. The camp is on the edge of a dramatic cliff, near the base of the escarpment, and has just three reed-covered tents. It is a vintage, pre-1940s-style camp with Tilley

Chongwe has something for everyone, with the sophisticated elegance of Chongwe House (above) in contrast to the rustic, close-to-nature pleasures of staying at Bushbuck (right). Chongwe River Camp (below) retains the atmosphere of an adventurer's camp.

lamps and bucket showers and it is just the sort of place to immerse in nature for a night or two.

I love rivers and with the Zambezi right on your doorstep there is the option of canoeing trips, boating and tiger fishing. Game viewing is also extremely rewarding. Forays into the Lower Zambezi National Park, which lies just across the Chongwe, include regular sightings of lion, wild dog, buffalo and leopard. There is also a great deal of wildlife at the back of the camp and the afternoon siestas are far from dull. Just about every day, just after lunch during the dry season, elephant bulls wander into camp. Their intention is not to thrill dozing guests (which they do), but to gorge themselves on albida fruit. These bright yellow offerings, which fall from the trees during the driest times of the year, are simply irresistible to elephant.

Chongwe River Camp (above right) is on the site used by explorers Livingstone and Selous. Bushbuck (above left) is further up the channel near a waterfall that spills off the escarpment.

The pods of a bushwillow (above) and a saddle-billed stork (above right).

Chris Liebenberg (right) remembers the days when he used to go on patrol in the park.

CONSERVING ZAMBIA'S NATURAL HERITAGE

'I always wanted to be in the bush,' says Christiaan Liebenberg. He and his father set up Chongwe River Camp in the 1990s when there were very few tourism operators in the Lower Zambezi and when poachers had the run of the place.

'In the early years poaching was terrible. Gunshots were going off all over the place and we used to go out for a few days at a time on patrol. Eventually my parents became concerned for my safety and persuaded me to stop.'

Chris and his father were founder members of Conservation Lower Zambezi in 1994, and this non-governmental organisation now provides support and training to the Zambian Wildlife Authority (ZAWA) patrols.

'Up to 100 elephants a year were being poached in the early days,' says Chris, 'now there are just one or two fatalities. Kudu are an indicator species of a healthy environment and the fact that there are so many of them bodes very well for this area.'

ROBIN POPE SAFARIS

South Luangwa
ZAMBIA

Robin Pope Safaris is the largest and most established operator in Zambia's famed Luangwa Valley and was a founder member of Classic Camps. When you stay in a bush camp (above left), or in the stunning Luangwa House (above right) or one of the other three camps, the emphasis of the guiding will always be on the fabulous nature found here – and getting up close and personal.

When Robin Pope went for his first interview as a guide he was interviewed by Norman Carr, widely regarded as the 'father' of Luangwa National Park. During the interview, Norman asked Robin to identify a bird flying overhead. The bird, a yellow-billed kite, was such an easy one to identify that Robin laughed ... and then failed the interview. A year later, he tried again and this time the story goes that a group of pipe-smoking hunters walked him once around a lagoon and proclaimed him a guide. Thirty years on, Robin is regarded as one of the best walking guides in Africa and has an uncanny ability to get people excited about anything, whether it is a lion, an impala or some bracket fungus. He has not lost his sense of humour either. 'Walking is like reading a book and game drives are like films,' says Robin, quoting a guest from one of his trails. As a photographer, I love a good film, but I know just what he means. Going on a walking trail with this quietly spoken, highly knowledgeable and much loved gentleman is an experience not to be missed and walks are often booked up years in advance.

Robin Pope Safaris is the largest operator in the Luangwa Valley and includes three main camps, two private villas and a mobile tented operation. Tena Tena, which is the flagship, was described by *The Times* as 'altogether beyond superlatives ... one of the best safari camps in the whole of Africa'. All of the camps are just as I like it: offering great food, comforts and functionality without being overly fussy. 'We like to keep our camps simple,' Robin confirms, 'and they must have a view into nature.' He is still very much part of the day-to-day running of the camps and the guides he has trained, mostly Zambian, share his passion for the bush, his gentlemanly manners and his extraordinary attention to detail.

The second ingredient of the RPS success story is Jo, a zoology graduate who arrived here 20 years ago (leaving behind London and a fiancé) with a mandate to help with the catering for 'a couple

of months'. It is widely acknowledged that her sense of fun and uncanny marketing ability is what put Robin Pope Safaris, Luangwa and indeed the whole of Zambia on the international safari map. Jo makes things happen and has even been instrumental in developing an airline in the valley for all operators.

In 2005 Jo deservedly won the Responsible Tourism Award (Individual Category) for her work with the development of schools in the community area bordering the park. The Kawaza School Fund, which she started, has received generous donations from guests and currently supports the wages of a number of teachers and over 50 students at various levels of secondary and tertiary education. It has

NKWALI. One of the few permanent lodges on the banks of the Luangwa River, Nkwali (top left and top right) offers the option of visiting during the Emerald Season. Heading off from here by boat (right) is always an adventure. Keep your binoculars handy for the small riverside dwellers, such as this malachite kingfisher (above).

also upgraded the facilities at two local schools, including providing desks and building classrooms.

Jo has also recently started the Reforest Nsefu project, which plants fast-growing trees to reforest areas where deforestation has already occurred, and these will hopefully prevent cutting down of hardwoods in the area. 'An interesting thing about trees,' says Jo, 'is that they release carbon when they are first planted and only offset a little carbon for the first few years. So the carbon offset portion of the project is concentrating on slow-growing fruit trees and agro-forestry species, which will benefit the local community and hopefully not be cut down.' They are also looking to plant other

Robin Pope (top left) has a remarkable knowledge of the area's wildlife and his guiding style has set the tone for the camps. Staying in a bush camp (top right and centre) is a memorable experience and perhaps the best way to get really close to nature. Elephant (above) are creatures of habit and follow the same routes year after year.

Carmine bee-eaters (above left) nest in the river's muddy banks during September and yellow-billed storks (above right) are often seen hunting fish in the flooded lagoons in February and March. Wild dog (right) are seen throughout the year.

A Luangwa diary

Robin Pope Safaris offers an opportunity to witness the change of seasons in this great game park all year round. The peak game viewing season is from May to October during the dry season, when game is forced to come and drink at the shrinking lagoons that are found on both sides of the main river. This is also a great time for birding, with crimson bee-eaters nesting in the river banks and also bird parties: these involve vast flocks of storks and pelicans that move from shrinking lagoon to lagoon feasting off the barbel that are trapped in the shallow mud. During this time guests can choose between staying at three main camps (Nkwali, Tena Tena and Nsefu) and it's also possible to go on mobile- and bush-camping trips.

The months of October and November are extremely hot and at some point will see the start of the rains. During the wet summers it is impossible to drive through much of the park and the camps at Tena Tena and Nsefu are completely dismantled. The RPS team and their guests are now confined to Nkwali, from where they watch the swollen, thick and brown river rushing past the camp. During this time, the so-called Emerald Season, it's a joy to be in the park and to go boating upstream to see heronries in the flooded lagoons. The summer landscape is gloriously green, the animals are relaxed and healthy and there are virtually no other visitors. It is, in some ways, my best time for photography and especially good for wild dog.

trees that can benefit the community, such as neem, which increases the fertility of the soil, and also jatropha, which can be used to make a natural bio-gas that can be utilised in lieu of paraffin.

South Luangwa is at the southern end of the Great Rift Valley and the wildly meandering river which forms its heart is uninterrupted by dams or bridges for its entire length of more than 700 kilometres. It is also staggeringly beautiful, with bird-filled lagoons, leopard (there are as many as two per square kilometre) as well as lion, elephant, puku, the endemic Thorneycroft giraffe and hundreds of species of birds. It has, largely as a result of Robin's guiding, become one of the best destinations for walking safaris in Africa. There is, of course, also the opportunity to explore the reserve in vehicles and, in summer, by boat.

Robin and Jo Pope live year-round at RoJo House – a dreamy thatched home on the banks of a lagoon next to the Luangwa River – a stone's throw from Nkwali, which is the headquarters and main camp of Robin Pope Safaris. If ever I could stay in one place and watch Africa's seasons change, this would be the spot. And it is not only because it gives year-round access to South Luangwa, one of the great game parks of Africa, but because every time I return I am reminded that it is the people of Zambia – and of RPS in particular – who make it such a special place to visit.

The historic Nsefu Camp has been fully restored and is situated in a prime game viewing area of the park.

TENA TENA (above and right) in the game-rich Nsefu section of South Luangwa is only open during the dry season. Sundowners are always a treat and are served from the bonnet of the game vehicle (top) or in special surprise locations such as Chichele Hill (centre), one of the highest points in the park.

BENGUERRA LODGE

MOZAMBIQUE

Benguerra Lodge

Bazaruto Archipelago

MOZAMBIQUE

Benguerra Lodge, situated in the Bazaruto Archipelago off the east coast of Mozambique, offers the pleasures of a remote tropical island escape. A romantic sunset cruise followed by a beach dinner (left) is a typical treat for honeymooners. High tea served on the lawns of the lodge (below left) and trips around the island (below centre) are also on offer.

Barefoot, salty and feeling hungry, we ended a morning snorkelling in the crystal-clear waters off Mozambique's Bazaruto Archipelago with a picnic. The glorious feast that had been set up by Benguerra Lodge comprised peri-peri prawns, fresh salads and ice-cold wine and was laid out beneath a wide terracotta-coloured awning on a deserted sandbar that jutted into blue tropical waters. 'Life,' I thought to myself, 'does not get much better than this.'

The Bazaruto Archipelago is southern Mozambique's greatest gem. It lies 24 kilometres offshore of Vilanculos and is part of a national park that includes the sand bars and tropical waters as well as the islands of Bazaruto, Benguerra, Magaruque, Santa Carolina and Banque.

Benguerra Lodge was the first to be established on the island and has wonderful suites built right on the beach, where you can watch lateen-rigged dhows slipping past the horizon just as they have done for hundreds of years. The experience is beyond words and then, of course, there are the long white beaches, tropical coral reefs and island pleasures that have made these islands

The Dhow Bar (above) is where guests gather to chat about their day fishing, snorkelling or diving.

The beachfront *casitas* (top) have plunge pools and private verandas that spill onto the beach.

so well known. Over the years, I have visited Benguerra Lodge six times and have always been overwhelmed by the hospitality of the staff, many of whom have worked at the lodge since inception. The Landrey family, which has run the lodge since 1989, has a background in the safari industry in Zimbabwe and much of the style is drawn from their experience, with the emphasis on great food, intimate hospitality and service.

The lodge is built mostly of hardwoods that have been imported from the mainland and the furniture and intricately carved doors have all been made using local craftsmen. The ideas for the lavish interiors with their rich red fabrics have been derived from Swahili influences. The lodge has evolved over the years in response to changing demands, but nobody could have foreseen the events that would come in February 2007 when a cyclone hit the island, destroying much of the forest, ripping the roof off the lodge and flattening many of the rooms. 'Most of all, we were sad about the forest,' said Margie Adcock, one of the founders, 'but we managed to save many of the trees by supporting them with ropes and it is great to see how they are recovering.'

Incredibly, the lodge reopened eight months later sporting 10 lavish *casitas*. They are remarkable places to stay, with lavish interiors, indoor and outdoor bathrooms, private plunge pools, and right on the water, with wide verandas where you can order private lunches. Other options at Benguerra still exist, including the private villa, which has two double rooms, a private pool, housekeeper, butler and chef, and also two cabanas and four children's rooms.

After dinner each evening (I enjoyed wonderful meals with a spicy mix of Morocco, East Africa and Mozambique) wake-up calls – and activities – are planned. Large kingfish and queenfish usually bite during the summer months and, weather and tide permitting, the two dedicated guides who work at the lodge encourage anglers to wake up early for the action.

Large copper baths, lavish bedrooms with carved doors and colourful décor, reflect influences from the Swahili coast.

ISLAND PLEASURES

'I can't believe the size of the fish in this place,' one angler from America told me after a day spent on the sea that had seen him catch a 35-kilogram kingfish. 'I just wish I had brought heavier tackle.' All fishing here is strictly catch and release.

Other activities include scuba diving, snorkelling on Two Mile Reef, trips to Pansy Island and also trips around the island. Benguerra is 11 kilometres long and five kilometres wide and has three inland freshwater lakes, which are home to myriad waterbirds and small populations of crocodile. As the island was once linked to the mainland, suni and duiker can often be spotted in the forests. Up to 150 species of birds may be seen, including lesser flamingo, terns, sandpipers, blue-cheeked bee-eater and crab plover. The surrounding waters constitute one of the last habitats of the highly endangered dugong, a slow-moving, seal-like aquatic mammal that lives in shallow waters and feeds exclusively on sea grass. It was dugongs that inspired the legends of mermaids – staying at Benguerra, such romantic notions do not feel entirely far-fetched.

Snorkellers on the surface at Two Mile Reef (top) where moray eels (above left) are found. Fly-fishing (above right) is offered and is all catch and release. The freshwater lakes on Benguerra Island (right).

A picnic (top) awaits guests after a diving or snorkelling excursion.

The outside showers in the *casitas* (right) feature mosaic floors and copper fittings.

Island life continues around the lodge (top). In addition to private pools, the *casitas* each have a hammock for relaxing and a shady sala on the beach. Benguerra Lodge offers guests a variety of treatments in a spa set deep in a shady forest.

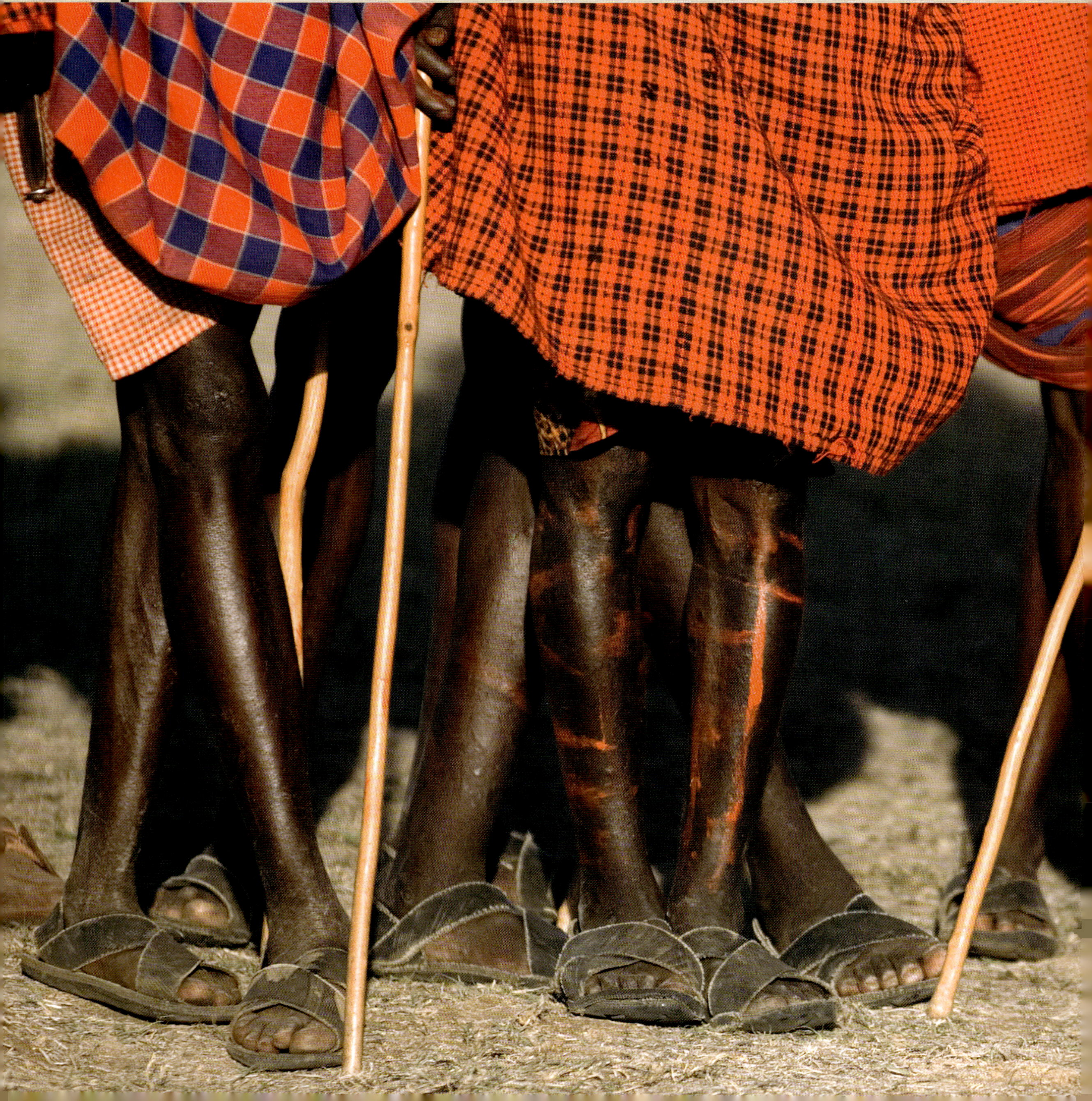

TANZANIA

Greystoke Mahale

Mahale Mountains National Park

TANZANIA

Greystoke Mahale (above) is built on the shores of Lake Tanganyika with the Mahale Mountains as its incredible backdrop. The mountains are home to groups of chimpanzee (below left). Often, during spells of perfect weather, dinner is set up on the sandy beach (below centre). Greystoke Mahale's bandas are beautifully designed and wildly exotic, built mostly out of the wooden beams, masts and hulls of old traditional dhows.

'The air is scented with jasmine, the forest rich, the water of the lake gin-clear and lightly chilled. And if I dare to put an imprint on this paradise I had better get it right.' So said Irish explorer Roland Purcell when he arrived on the shores of Lake Tanganyika in the 1980s.

He had set foot in one of the most remote places in the world. And, on the slopes of the 2 500-metre-high Mahale Mountains, his only neighbours were some 1 000 chimpanzees – the largest known population anywhere in the world.

Greystoke Mahale lodge, which Purcell built at the foot of the mountains, is like none other. The main mess is spectacular and stands on the beach, with its soaring prow-like wings, and its upper deck is the perfect vantage point to look out over the lake. The bandas are open-fronted and are situated on the edge of the forest looking out over the soft sandy beach; the interiors are designed with flair and passion.

At the end of the dry season in October, the chimps spend most of their time on the lower slopes of the mountains and we saw them on every walk. The lodge was strict about the viewing protocol, which has been devised for Mahale Mountains National Park by an international team of scientists, doctors and veterinarians to protect the chimpanzees and their forest. Viewing groups are limited to six people for just one hour a day and a 10-metre distance must be maintained at all times. Once the chimps brushed right past us on the path and we spent time with them on

The lodge is inaccessible by road, so guests are flown to a small airstrip and then taken down the waters of Lake Tanganyika by dhow ... a languid and peaceful 90-minute journey that sets the pace of your stay at Greystoke Mahale.

THE MIRACLE OF AFRICA'S DEEPEST LAKE

Lake Tanganyika is 720 kilometres long, 70 kilometres wide and up to 1 440 metres deep (the second deepest in the world to Lake Baikal in Russia, which is the deepest), and holds one-sixth of the world's fresh water. The water is alkaline, with minimal algae growth, and as a result it is fantastically clear. On still days it is like a mirror, but the wind can quickly whip up the water into waves. On the lake it is possible to go kayaking or exploring by dhow. With some 260 species of endemic cichlid (say 'sicklid'), a freshwater jellyfish, hippo and an abundance of birds, the lake is full of life.

the forest floor. We came to recognise the family groups, dominant males, cute babies and the characters amongst them. I developed something of a connection with Darwin, a pale-faced, freckled young male who always appeared deep in thought. There were also vervet and colobus monkey, as well as bushbuck, bushpig, leopard and amazing birds, including red-chested sunbird, blue-breasted bee-eater, yellow-rumped tinkerbird, olive pigeon and tambourine dove.

One afternoon we went out on the lake and chugged slowly across the mirror-like surface. We stopped to enjoy the silence and I was thrilled to spot a water cobra slipping beneath a rock. These snakes hunt fish underwater, but are extremely shy of people.

Life felt easy back at the lodge. We lived barefoot with sand beneath our feet, wore bathing costumes and sarongs, and ate sushi so fresh that it would have satisfied even the most discerning castaway. Going to sleep at night we were lulled by the gentle lapping of waves. Greystoke would have loved the place – I certainly did.

Whilst staying at Greystoke Mahale, there are water-based activities such as fishing, as well as forest treks. Several chimp families (top) have been studied since 1965 and have become accustomed to humans. The open-fronted bandas (below and right) are on the edge of the forest, but you can still hear the gentle lapping of the lake as you drift off to sleep.

Sand Rivers Selous

Selous Game Reserve

TANZANIA

Selous is about big mammals and even bigger landscapes. Hippo (below left) and elephant (below right) are regularly seen on game drives. Birders, too, are in for a treat and stand a good chance of seeing African skimmers (above) along the Rufiji River.

The Selous Game Reserve extends over more than 50 000 square kilometres (over three times larger than the Serengeti). It is the largest conservation reserve in Africa and part of the Selous Niassa Ecosystem, which extends for 155 000 square kilometres through much of southern Tanzania and northern Mozambique.

'When I began safaris here more than 20 years ago,' says Richard Bonham, 'I travelled the length of this amazing reserve on my portaged walking safaris. But always I found myself returning to the Sand Rivers area with its variety of terrain and its ever-reliable game. When we finally decided to create Sand Rivers Selous, it was obvious where we should settle.'

Bonham settled in style. The stone-and-thatch lodge has five standard rooms and two suites. All are open-fronted and look out over the Rufiji River. The suites have a separate lounge area and small plunge pool. There is a large swimming pool at the main mess.

A recent addition to Sand Rivers Selous is The Rhino House. This exclusive one-bedroom 'honeymoon' cottage is the perfect private hideaway: meals are served in your own dining area, and there is a small pool for an afternoon of chilling out, plus your own car and guide to take you out for daily adventures. This home for two offers total bush bliss, day and night, and the greatest luxury of all, a private piece of the great beyond.

Guests can enjoy sundowners on the deck whilst taking in the magnificent view across the river with hippo wallowing in the waters below.

At Sand Rivers Selous you can expect long lunches, candle-lit dinners and romantic sundowners, but the traditional safari element is never far away. The lodge's famous Selous Walking Safaris take people out on foot into this incredible reserve. On a boating trip up the Rufiji River we pulled onto the shore near Steigler's Gorge and had a cookout of bacon and eggs on the beach. I also went on a fly-camp beside the shimmering waters of Lake Tagalala. The square 'rooms' were made of mosquito netting and had separate changing tents, toilets and hot showers. Dinner was served at a table beneath the stars, with grunting hippo, roaring lion and hyena as our wild companions.

Bonham was inspired and assisted by Bimb and Lizzy Theobald when he started Sand Rivers Selous. They shared a deep concern for the decimation of thousands of black rhino in this vast reserve during the 1970s and together they started the Selous Rhino Trust. This has now been running for more than 10 years and the 16 black rhino that have been identified suggest that, thanks to conservation, their numbers are at last recovering.

The interiors at Sand Rivers Selous are a natural extension of the environment and game drives and boat trips allow guests a closer look into this incredible reserve.

Sand Rivers Selous is situated on the banks of the Rufiji River (top) and all the rooms and suites look out onto the water. Hippo and crocodile are resident here, but a large variety of other game can be seen in the area, including hyena and wild dog.

Tortilis camp & Elsa's kopje & Joy's camp &
Governors' camps & Loldia house & Mfangano island camp
& Cottars safari camp & Loisaba wilderness

KENYA

Giraffe with Kilimanjaro backdrop – the quintessential view from Amboseli.

TORTILIS CAMP

Amboseli National Park

KENYA

The tents at Tortilis (below left) are reminiscent of traditional East African safaris with bathrooms built onto the back. The pool (below right) is a welcome asset during the hot summer months. On balmy evenings, meals are served on the veranda (below centre) overlooking a floodlit waterhole.

Long lines of thirsty elephant walking across a dry, dusty moonscape beneath the imposing form of snow-topped Kilimanjaro have become one of the quintessential images of Africa. It has also made Amboseli, which is the place to see this unforgettable sight, the second-most visited park in Kenya after the Masai Mara. Tortilis Camp, just outside the reserve in a 30 000-hectare private concession owned by the local Masai, is away from the crowds and is the most exclusive way to experience the drama.

Tortilis's 17 classic safari tents are all set in the shade of a string of umbrella-shaped *Acacia tortilis* trees, only a stone's throw from the game beyond. They have patios, *en suite* bathrooms, great style and traditional safari-style character. The gardens attract brightly coloured shrikes and many other birds and there is also a crystal-clear swimming pool. A stylish house, with two large *en suite* rooms and lavish living areas, caters for families and small groups.

Stefano Cheli, Tortilis co-owner, is the grandson of an accomplished Italian chef (his grandfather won the Golden Oyster for best seafood restaurant in Italy) and is himself a serious foodie who says that his camps provide the best lodge food in

Most of the staff (above) are employed from the local Masai community and they are wonderful hosts and guides. The tents (right) are set in a garden beneath the tortilis trees that give the camp its name.

From a tent to Tortilis – and beyond

Stefano Cheli and Liz Peacock – from Italy and England respectively – started out doing mobile safaris in the 1980s.

'We stayed in a pup tent in our friend's garden,' says Stefano. 'We had canvas tents, two vehicles and a massive overdraft.'

In the early 1990s they started their first camp, which was Tortilis. Today, the camp provides income for more than 500 Masai living in the area.

In 1996 Tortilis won the Tourism for Tomorrow Award for its conservation efforts, and was given certification from Kenya's ecotourism society for being proactive in responsible tourism. It has also been listed among *Condé Nast*'s elite Gold List Awards. Today, in addition to Tortilis Camp in Amboseli National Park, Stefano Cheli and Liz Peacock have camps in Meru National Park (Elsa's Kopje), the Masai Mara (Elephant Pepper Camp) and in Shaba National Reserve (Joy's Camp).

Kenya. I have visited many lodges and I would say that Tortilis is definitely in the running for the best lodge food anywhere in Africa. The pasta is all home-made and the recipes for risotto, linguine and spaghetti have been perfected over the years.

'Our family came from Bologna so we know all about sauces,' says Stefano. 'My mother personally trained chefs like Joseph Nkwachet, whose son is now at Joy's Camp, to make things the real Italian way. We promise that you are not going to get a sauce with ketchup or any chemicals in it. The secret is in the ingredients and the lodge has an established vegetable garden where the chef is able to select the freshest herbs and salads.'

From the dining area and the sundowner decks there is a glorious view over a waterhole frequented by elephant, buffalo, wildebeest and other game and beyond to the towering massif of Kilimanjaro. Tortilis itself enjoys the freedom of the concession area bordering the park and here visitors are permitted to go on guided walks, which are privileges not permitted in national parks.

Amboseli means 'salty dust' and much of its surface is strewn with volcanic ash. Trees, particularly acacias, are plentiful in the vicinity of springs, which draw wildebeest, zebra, hartebeest and lion. And at the heart of the park is the lake,

which is mostly dry, but provides a spectacular canvas for photography.

The elephants of Amboseli are some of the most relaxed in Africa, and this is largely thanks to the American scientist Cynthia Moss and her team of elephant researchers, who studied them constantly for more than 25 years and are still doing so today. One particular herd, led by matriarch Echo, has been the subject of several BBC wildlife films, including *Echo* and its sequel *The Next Generation*. Images taken by cinematographer Martyn Colbech are generously displayed. at the lodge.

Like all mountains, Kilimanjaro is often hidden behind cloud so you need to be lucky and also patient to capture its true glory. I can't wait to get back there and try for myself to capture an image of Africa's largest mammals pictured against its highest landmass.

Walking safaris (above) are one of the highlights of a stay at Tortilis.

The lodge is renowned for its wonderful food and the herb and vegetable gardens (left) provide the freshest of ingredients. Relaxing with a book at Tortilis House (below).

Elsa's Kopje

Meru National Park

KENYA

The swimming pool at Elsa's, like the lodge, is perched on the edge of a granite hill and has commanding views over the plains of the Meru National Park.

Great effort was made to ensure that Elsa's blended with its rocky surroundings (above). From the main dining area paths lead around the tumbled granite to the exquisite bedrooms.

Meru National Park has the largest diversity of species than any other park and includes northern as well as southern species. Driving in the park it is possible to pass from savanna (below centre), through woodlands, palm and riverine forests and into wetlands in a single outing.

Just 10 kilometres north of the equator, on the top of the tumbled granite outcrop called Mughwango Hill, is Elsa's Kopje – a lodge with 360-degree views over the plains of Meru National Park in northern Kenya. It is a place with wide vistas and such imaginative architecture that it immediately captures your heart. It has also played a very important role in the conservation of Meru National Park.

Meru is part of a conservation area that covers 1 500 square kilometres and includes the adjoining Kora, Rahole and Bisanadi reserves, and it lies northeast of Mount Kenya and east of the Nyambeni Mountains in an extremely isolated part of northern Kenya. The park became famous for its association with George Adamson and during its heyday there were thousands of visitors a year. In the 1990s, however, organised bands of poachers had taken out so much of its wildlife to supply the bush meat trade that Kenya Wildlife Services were at the point of de-proclaiming the park. It was during these difficult times that Stefano Cheli and Liz Peacock started negotiations with Kenya Wildlife Services to establish a lodge. Four years later they had the approval and in 1999 they opened Elsa's Kopje.

'Elsa's is still the largest investment in the park and we believe that our commitment played a major role in ensuring that it was not de-gazetted and turned into rice fields,' says Stefano.

Another turning point for Meru came in 2000 when Mark Jenkins was appointed warden. He used funding obtained internationally to train patrols and was also responsible for reintroducing large numbers of game back into the park. These included black and white rhino and the rare and endangered Grevy's zebra.

Elsa's Kopje is an incredible achievement considering the landscape and the nature of the lodge. Its eight cottages are built from natural

materials and blend in so beautifully with the environment that the rocks and trees have become part of the furniture. Some of the rooms have trees growing through them, boulders form part of the walls, and they are all quite different. I was most taken by room number two, where a stream of hot water trickled for some five metres from the tap, over the rocks, and finally into the bath. Another feature is a 15-metre-wide suspension bridge that leads guests over a gorge to two of the rooms.

The newest addition to the lodge is a private house on the eastern side of the hill that is ideal for families. There is also a romantic honeymoon suite, which has been built on three different levels, and includes a private dining deck, a lounge and a bedroom with more forever views.

The House (above) has its own swimming pool, kitchen and lounge ... a wonderful retreat for two couples or for small families. Rock agamas (right) are one of the creatures that live in the rocks alongside the lodge.

The Story of Elsa

George Adamson and his beloved Elsa.

George Adamson, the 'lion man' of Africa, was one of the founders of wildlife conservation in Kenya. His original camp is just below the present-day Elsa's Kopje. It was here that George, along with Joy Adamson, released Elsa, the orphaned lioness, back into the wild. The remarkable story is chronicled through the book *Born Free,* which was written by Joy and became a successful film in 1966 starring Virginia McKenna and Bill Travers. After the Adamsons' separation, George continued for a short while in Meru, but was transferred to Kora National Reserve where he died at the hands of poachers. Joy was killed under mysterious circumstances in 1980 in Shaba (see page 118).

Their legacies have continued. Virginia McKenna, who played Joy Adamson in the film, was so influenced by the experience of working with the Adamsons in Africa that she started the Born Free Foundation, a highly successful fund-raising organisation that reintroduces orphaned animals back into the wild. She is still drawn to Africa and is a regular visitor to Elsa's Kopje.

'I have left my heart here once again,' she wrote in the visitors' book on 24 September 2006. 'It is wonderful to know that Elsa's is still in such caring, kind and generous hands. Elsa, George and Joy are still here.'

Sitting in the lodge beside the infinity pool watching the blue water melt into the sky, or on your private balcony, it is hard to believe that there are any other people in the world let alone any difficulties in it.

On lazy summer days it is a great idea to take a picnic down to the river and possibly throw a line into the water. The park has 13 rivers which run from west to east, including the Tana, which is the largest in Kenya. The rich diversity of Meru includes more than 350 bird species and game typical to northern Kenya, such as buffalo, lion and leopard, as well as Grevy's zebra, gerenuk, Somali ostrich, reticulated giraffe and lesser kudu.

'For me,' says Stefano, 'true wilderness is being able to stop on the top of a hill and enjoy a gin and tonic. Racing around looking for the Big Five is very depressing and sad,' he adds.

I heeded his words and walked to the top of the Mughwango Hill. The wide open spaces unfolded below and I thought of the history of the park, how Adamson once camped here with his beloved Elsa, and the long road that the park had taken back towards recovery.

Elsa's is famous for its endless views and the way the lodge merges into its rocky environment (above and below). The upstairs lounge of the Honeymoon House (left).

Joy's Camp

Shaba National Reserve

KENYA

The Ewaso Ngiro River (above right) is fringed by doum palms and forms the northern boundary of Shaba National Reserve. Much of the design inspiration for the camp has been derived from the influence of the Somali and Borana people who live in this part of northern Kenya. Walks along the dramatic gorge formed by the Ewaso Ngiro River can be enjoyed and a sundowner at the end of the day is the perfect way to unwind.

In Kenya, the meandering Ewaso Ngiro River wends its way through a spectacular landscape of waving blonde grasslands, rolling hills, palms and riverine forest on its way to the Lorian Swamps. A trio of parks, namely Buffalo Springs, Samburu and Shaba National Park, have been established here in the so-called Northern Frontier to conserve an arid wilderness where dryland species such as Grevy's zebra, reticulated giraffe, gerenuk, Beisa oryx and Somali ostrich may be seen alongside elephant, buffalo, lion, cheetah, the diminutive dik-dik, and many other species.

Shaba, which is the least visited and largest of the three parks, covers 239 square kilometres and is named after the Shaba Hills that form its western boundary. The Ewasa Ngiro River flows for 34 kilometres along its northern boundary and there are also 17 natural springs, a magnet for game in a region that experiences just 300 millimetres of rainfall per annum.

It was on the fringe of one of these springs, within sight of the Shaba Hills, that Joy Adamson made her home in the 1970s – and it was also here where she died under mysterious circumstances in 1980. She chose a prime spot in the park and it is at this very same place, under the shade of a grove of *Acacia tortilis* trees and overlooking a wetland with a parade of buffalo, ostrich and other game, where Stefano Cheli and Mike Lawrence have built Joy's Camp more than three decades later.

For more than 20 years both Stefano and Mike had been taking safaris into Shaba, which was their favourite part of Kenya, and it was always Stefano's dream to build a camp here. Many people thought they were taking a chance building in such a remote area, but it has worked wonderfully.

The 10 lavish tents each comprise 100 square metres of billowing pale canvas, screed floors, wide balconies, king-sized beds, and bright lemon, green and orange fabrics that decorate the generous interiors. The dining area, too, is a mix of canvas

The camp, with its warm colours and inspired design ideas, is a remarkable place to stay and is in one of the most remote parts of Kenya. The pool (top) is especially welcome during the hot summer months.

The Queen of Shaba

Joy's Camp is built on the site that was originally Joy Adamson's home in Shaba National Park. The author and naturalist, who was born Friederike Gessner in 1910 to a wealthy Austrian family, spent more than 40 years in Kenya. She was an accomplished artist and did some 700 paintings, many of which are now housed at the National Museum in Nairobi. She wrote nine books, including *Born Free*, which was turned into a Hollywood movie that helped put East Africa on the map. In 1977 she moved to Shaba in order to rehabilitate and release Penny the leopard, the heroine of her last published book, *Queen of Shaba*.

In early January 1980 Joy stumbled in from the wilderness, bleeding from her wounds. Initially it was assumed that lions had attacked her, but a youth was later found guilty. The Joy Adamson Museum at Joy's Camp includes an old typewriter, manuscripts and a photograph of her meeting the Queen of England amongst the interesting memorabilia. There is also a plaque that commemorates the spot where she died.

and concrete with graceful arches, gleaming copper and elegant furniture. Shaba is the land of the Somali and Borana people and it is from the cultural melting pot of these people that much of the inspiration for the lodge has been derived.

The camp has an extremely gentle footprint. Battery banks and solar heaters in the tents ensure that minimal electricity is consumed and all the laundry is done by hand and dried in the sun. Garbage is also removed weekly by truck. More than 60 per cent of the staff is employed from local communities. Many of them were previously cattle herders, but as with all the Cheli and Peacock camps, they have been trained to offer personal service and to prepare the simple and wholesome Italian home-style cooking that has become the Stefano Cheli signature.

Mike died on 18 August 2006, one month after his camp was opened. His favourite tent, where he spent a night before he died, was renamed 'Chief's Tent' in his honour. A school that has been built some 20 kilometres from the lodge and a pipeline that brings life-giving water from a spring in the park to the many pastoralists living in the area is also a testimony to his work in the area.

The dryland specials found in this part of East Africa include the Somali ostrich (left) and Grevy's zebra (above). Birdlife, too, is prolific.

The tents at Joy's Camp (top) are very spacious and have large balconies where guests can watch game coming to drink at the springs in front of the lodge.

Governors' Camps

Masai Mara

KENYA

Governors' offers the quintessential East African safari with balloon trips over the Mara (opposite) being a speciality. It is a wonderful experience that ends with a champagne breakfast on the plains. Walking safaris are also offered (above left) for a more down-to-earth experience. After a game drive guests return to Little Governors' Camp (above right) for a romantic fireside dinner.

It is amazing to think that in 1972 nobody had ever thought of building a luxury permanent tented safari camp. In that year, Aris Grammaticas, the Tanzanian-born son of a Greek railway engineer, secured a concession in the northwestern Masai Mara National Reserve and announced to a somewhat sceptical public that he was going to open a camp with 'large tented rooms with big bathrooms on the back'. Aris called it Governors' because it was in the prime game viewing area on the forested bank of the Mara River, which was a site reserved exclusively for colonial governors and their guests, and he set about recreating a typical safari experience of old. Wildlife and photographic tourism was in its infancy in Kenya at that time (there was only one other lodge in the entire Mara), but Aris felt confident and slowly but surely managed to convince tourists from his small offices in Nairobi to come and see the Masai Mara.

The rest, as they say, is history and today Governors' has four camps in the Mara and three others on Lake Victoria, Lake Naivasha and in the foothills of Rwanda's Virunga Mountains. Aris and his two sons and daughter – Dominic, Justin and Ariana – now employ close on 600 people and support numerous charities, schools, community support projects (such as the world's first bio-gas plant in Masai Manyatta) and an eye clinic.

I started my journey at the Mara where it all began, in an area a BBC Natural History director has described as 'the best wildlife real estate in the world'. Aside from its being close to the main points where the famous wildebeest migration crosses the Mara River, the greatest asset of the Governors' area is its proximity to the Musiara Swamp, which lies just behind the camps – arguably the best game viewing area in the Mara ecosystem. The action here is sometimes unbelievable. Once whilst watching two terrified snarling lionesses that were treed by a herd of buffalo, a lone leopard prowled into view. It was hard to know where to look next. And don't be surprised to see some of the best wildlife photographers in the world right here capturing the action. Conservationist Jonathan Scott bases

GOVERNORS' CAMP. **The original Governors' Camp, sited where colonial governors once camped, is a place for everyone to experience the romance of East Africa. Dinners (above) are served by waiters who have been working here for three decades and the tents (right) are equally welcoming.**

Lion (below) and other predators follow the migration.

himself at Governors' and all the footage from the award-winning BBC documentary the *Big Cat Diaries* is filmed here.

Governors' Camp, Little Governors' Camp, Governors' Il Moran Camp and Governors' Private Camp, which make up the Governors' Camp Collection in the Mara, are all within a few kilometres of each other, but the forest is so thick that they are all totally private. Aris anticipated that the Mara would become popular one day and it is fortunate that his contract stipulates that no other developers may build within a 12-kilometre radius of Governors' Camp!

Governors' Camp has a prime position with views overlooking the Mara River and herds of wildebeest may often be seen on the plains. It is the largest of the camps, with 37 *en suite* tents, spacious gardens, and a fun, relaxed and very informal atmosphere. A waiter I met had worked here for 20 years (a recurring theme at all Governors' camps!) and the management was typically extremely experienced. In this case, the host was the highly regarded ornithologist, author and photographer Dave Richards.

Little Governors' Camp is on the far side of the Mara River and guests are pulled across in a small rowing boat. It is an intimate camp with just

LITTLE GOVERNORS' CAMP. **An adventurous boat ride takes guests over the Mara River to Little Governors' Camp. The camp (below) is on a spectacular wetland with large canvas tents (right) and hissing gas lamps that recall the traditional safari experience.**

THE GREATEST WILDLIFE SHOW ON EARTH

Rainfall and the availability of grazing triggers the migration of three million ungulates across the 27 000 square kilometres of the Serengeti Mara Ecosystem each year. It is undoubtedly one of the great natural wonders of the world and nowhere is it more spectacular than in the Mara, where the animals gather from July to October. At this time, the vast herds are not only in enormous concentrations, but they are forced to cross rocky and crocodile-infested rivers. Seeing the animals gathering, massing and finally diving into the waters was one of the most dramatic wildlife events of my life.

Governors' is near two major crossing points and I saw two crossings in as many days. 'In 2006 we saw close to 100 000 animals crossing in front of Governors' Camp,' one of the guides told me. 'It went on for more than three hours.'

17 tents that encircle a wetland bejewelled with lilies and frequented by buffalo and elephant.

Il Moran is the most luxurious camp and has 10 tented suites, each with a king-sized bed made from the gnarled and twisted stems of fallen ancient olive trees. From my deck, I gazed down over the Mara River and could see hippo wallowing in the water and crocodile basking on the banks.

Governors' also operates Governors' Private Camp, which is the smallest with just eight tents, and as the name suggests is reserved exclusively for individual groups.

Whichever camp you choose, each provides the authentic safari camp feel that has made Governors' such a success – with the emphasis always being on what happens outside the tent. People love it here and so does the *Sunday Times,* which listed Governors' as the 'best wilderness experience in the world'.

I fell asleep after a great adventure on the African plains, listening to animal, owl and insect calls drifting through the thin canvas walls of my tent. I have always loved sleeping in a tent and it was wonderful to consider that the whole notion of it started here.

Guided walks (above) on the northern boundary of the reserve, which is unfenced from the main park, allows guests to get close to nature.

The generously proportioned tented suites at Il Moran (below) have oversized beds and the largest bathrooms you are likely to find in any tented camp.

LOLDIA HOUSE

Lake Naivasha

KENYA

Loldia offers a wonderful taste of colonial East Africa in the heart of the Great Rift Valley. Guests usually head out for the day to Lake Nakuru, which is famed for its flamingos (above). Back at the lodge they are welcomed by Peter Njoroge (below left).

On the shores of Kenya's Lake Naivasha – the highest and purest of the string of great lakes that line the Great Rift Valley – is Loldia House, a delightful home shaded by fig trees, fringed by forests of fever trees, and with manicured gardens that stretch down to the lake. Loldia means 'wild dog' in Masai and, although you can no longer see these rare predators, it is still a wild place where buffalo and hippo gather on the wide lawns in front of the house.

It was at Loldia that the Hopcraft family settled in the early 1900s – and the rickety wagon in which they travelled from Nairobi still stands as a memory of that journey. The house itself was built by Italian prisoners of war during the 1940s.

Aris Grammaticas of Governors' Camps opened Loldia as a small hotel in the late 1980s and handpicked Peter Njoroge from one of the best restaurants in Kenya to run the place. Nearly two decades later, he is still doing so with aplomb. It was no wonder that the British *Tatler* named him 'Best Butler in the World'.

Loldia has a boat and Lake Naivasha begged to be explored – and within a short drive I could reach the steaming geysers of Hell's Gate and more than one million flamingos on Lake Nakuru. Slightly further away but still accessible is Lake Bogoria, famous for its geysers and flamingos.

Nakuru and its staggeringly beautiful vistas of blue waters and pink feathers made it so worth the journey. We spent the day patrolling the lake and fever tree forests that are famous for leopard, and saw a variety of game, including buffalo, eland, leopard and rhino.

Mfangano Island Camp

Lake Victoria

KENYA

When Prince and Princess Michael of Kent visited Governors' in the Masai Mara in the early 1980s, they asked owner Aris Grammaticas if he could recommend a place for some fishing, birding and relaxing. He took them to Mfangano Island on the eastern shores of Lake Victoria and the company has since built a small six-roomed lodge beneath a tall canopy of sycamore figs. There are daily flights to and from the Mara and guests can stay for the day – or overnight – to enjoy the changing light and moods of Africa's largest lake.

At 68 800 square kilometres this is also the world's second largest freshwater lake. First charted by Arab traders in 1160 CE, it was British explorer John Speke who proposed in 1858 that he had found the source of the Nile. This was confirmed some years later by the American explorer Henry Stanley.

With no other hotels, no roads and only fishermen as neighbours, the peacefulness is a sure thing. You can catch a Nile perch, visit fishing villages, relax at the pool or simply gaze at the lake as dhows slip slowly by. The gardens are a riot of colourful strelitzias, lilies and aloes and are filled with bronze sunbirds, black-headed gonoleks, double-toothed barbets and many other birds.

The rooms are in the style of the local Luo fishermen, with walls of smoothed plaster and clay and roofs of thatch and banana leaves. They all have views of the lake, but none so fine as the lavishly decorated Victorian Suite, which has a bed and bath that virtually hang over the water.

Most guests come here from other Governors' properties to enjoy a totally different water experience, where they can relax by the pool and go boating or fishing. The gardens at the lodge are lush and attract many species of birds whilst the lodge itself is set beneath the fig trees on the shores of the lake. Dinners are served out on the jetty, where guests can watch the twinkle of stars on the surface of the water.

Cottars 1920s Safari Camp

Masai Mara

KENYA

This antique wood-sided safari vehicle (opposite), used on sundowner outings, embodies the very spirit of this historical camp.

The views from the safari tents (above) stretch over Kenya and Tanzania. After a game outing seeing cheetah (below right) and other great game, Cottars guests return to a fine dining experience (below left).

When Theodore Roosevelt visited Africa in 1909, he defined the future of safaris, which would, forever afterwards, be associated with canvas, dust, wild animals and adventure. Chas Cottar was so inspired with the notion that he came to Africa and set up Cottars Safari Services in 1919. More than 80 years later Cottars is the longest established safari business in Africa and is run by Calvin Cottar, great-grandson of the intrepid Chas.

Cottars 1920s Safari Camp is in a private 22 000-acre reserve in the southeasternmost corner of the Masai Mara ecosystem, between the Masai Mara, Serengeti and Loliondo reserves. This private concession leased from the Masai community is in a mountainous region fed by springs and frequented by a profusion of game. Not only does Cottars include all the species found in the Mara (the migration passes through here), it also includes Schalow's turaco, colobus monkey, Chandler's reedbuck, wild dog and many other species that are not found elsewhere in the region. The wilderness atmosphere is more akin to the vast Serengeti and, because there is so little vehicle traffic, it is also possible to drive off-road for awesome game sightings.

Cottars 1920s Safari Camp is built mostly of canvas – with the exception of the bathrooms, which are a cement-on-hessian construction

resembling a Masai *manyatta* (homestead) – and is filled with fascinating memorabilia, including candelabra, leather trunks and rattan desks, many of which are heirlooms passed down through the Cottar family. There are also fold-up beds, original basins, an His Master's Voice-style gramophone and records and even an old-fashioned wooden safari vehicle that is used to transfer guests to and from the airport. The canvas walls of the tents are adorned with pictures of four generations of Cottars travelling in heavily laden safari trucks over rickety bridges and enjoying other thrills of the early days of safari.

Cottars has two camps, both of which are on a hill, with mountains behind and views towards the Serengeti. The main camp has six tents, which sleep just 12 guests, and the river camp has four tents, each accommodating four or five people. Four-course meals served on the finest crockery, with elegant cutlery and crystal glasses, are the norm here. And butlers are on hand at both camps to provide discreet, yet attentive service.

Cottars lounge (left) is filled with memorabilia and photographs collected over nearly a century by this pioneering safari family.

The Cottar legacy

Cottars is the longest established safari company in Africa, registered in British East Africa in 1919 by Chas Cottar and operated by him and his sons, Bud, Mike and Ted, during the twenties, thirties and forties. It was taken over by Mike's son Glen and his wife Pat in the fifties and they ran it until Calvin and Louise took over in the nineties.

'We are not in the safari business just for the sake of business,' says Calvin. 'This is our way to continue living in the land we love and our preferred way of life. We work hard to keep the vital essence of safaris alive and evoke the unchanging atmosphere of the Africa of the 1920s, the heyday of early explorers.'

Having lived with the Masai for 80 years, the Cottar family has noticed the decline in wildlife numbers and the increasing number of poor people living on the fringe of the Mara. They have set up the Cottars Conservation Trust, which leases land from the local community and ensures that they receive income from wildlife and are therefore more likely to support it. The Trust also supports schools, provides bursaries and funds teacher salaries, and finances medicines, an ambulance service and training in husbandry, bee-keeping and anti-poaching.

Four generations of Cottar men have been guiding in Africa. First (right to left) came Charles, followed by Mike, then Bud and Glen.

All the guides are handpicked by Calvin and include some of the most highly ranked in Kenya. The days are flexible and it is possible to go on guided walks, game drives, fishing trips and even an invigorating swim in a pool fed by a waterfall. Not surprisingly, this stylish and yet very simple camp has featured extensively in *Vogue*, *Architectural Digest* and Condé Nast *Traveller* and has won a succession of awards, including the best tented camp in the world. Calvin Cottar has been chosen as one of the top five safari guides in Africa by *Travel and Leisure* and voted as the best guide in Kenya by John Warburton-Lee. As Lucia van der Post writes in the *London Financial Times*: 'For those who find themselves hooked on Africa, there comes a time when they want something different, something lonelier and wilder ... Calvin Cottar and his 1920s safaris come with [that] kind of pedigree and promise.'

I have stayed in many camps in Africa, but none has inspired my imagination more than this camp – and I am sure that Roosevelt would have loved the place.

The River Camp at Cottars has spacious family tents complete with antique safari beds. The Cottars concession, which has the Sand River (below) as its boundary with the Masai Mara, is an excellent game viewing area with very few other guests. Guided walks with armed scouts are a must.

LOISABA WILDERNESS

Laikipia Plateau

KENYA

Loisaba is on the edge of the Laikipia Plateau and the rooms and house (above right) lord over a vast landscape with distant Mount Kenya visible on a clear day. For a real bird's-eye view, you need to take a trip in the lodge's hot-air balloon (above left).

The cliff-side pool at Loisaba House (opposite).

On the fringe of Kenya's northern frontier and covering approximately 800 000 hectares of wild savanna is the Laikipia Plateau. Fed by the Ewaso Ngiro and Engare Narok rivers, its rich grasslands and woodlands support all of the Big Five, including thousands of elephant and black rhino, plus wild dog, Grevy's zebra, reticulated giraffe, Jackson's hartebeest and more than 260 species of birds.

In the 1960s an Italian count named Carletto Ancilotto came to Kenya on safari and fell in love with the place and its wide views. He called his farm Colcheccio (a rude rendition of 'I told you so' in Italian) and quickly proved to his disbelieving friends back home that he could run a ranch in Africa where cattle and buffalo shared the same waterholes. When the Count began to age and lose interest in the ranch in the mid-1990s, his daughter Luisa negotiated a long lease on the land with a dynamic group of young Kenyans led by manager Tom Silvester. When they took over the ranch they renamed it Loisaba, or 'Seven Stars'. Through a commercial operation and the Loisaba Community Trust the ranch has focused on building up a model for sustainable development and ecotourism (see box page 137).

Tom, his wife and two children share a bush home near the Loisaba airstrip with a young reticulated giraffe, a Thomson's gazelle, two eagle owls and a host of other orphaned animals. Tom is a large-hearted man, but he leaves the hosting to his team of local warriors, all of whom are dressed in traditional clothing. An exceedingly friendly young Masai met me at the airport with a single red rose on top of his head. 'Samburu means "butterfly", after their penchant for dressing up,' explained Tom when I asked if this was for real, 'and the Laikipiak Masai have inherited many of the Samburu customs. You should see all the tinsel and decorations that they wear at Christmas time!'

Loisaba Lodge is built of stone, cedar and thatch high on the edge of a plateau, with breathtaking

The Laikipiak Masai have absorbed much Samburu custom into their flamboyant style of dress and serve at the lodge as guides and hosts (right and far right). The camel trails are one of the initiatives that benefit the local community. The setting of the lodge dining table (below) takes your breath away.

views towards Mount Kenya. Originally the home of the Count, it retains the air of a gentleman's manor with its wide leather sofas, large fireplaces, reading rooms, and seven luxury bedrooms with French doors that open to the same incredible views. It has indigenous gardens, tennis court, croquet lawn, bocce playing area, swimming pool, and a spa.

Loisaba House, a grand stone-and-thatched home built for part-owners Jim and Lori Denooyer, is a great place for families. Its artworks have been gathered across Africa, and the cliff-side swimming pool is one of the most remarkable places for a dip that I have ever seen. Eight kilometres away lies Loisaba Cottage, an even more relaxed hideaway with three suites and a private swimming pool.

Loisaba is 150 square kilometres, the same size as the Ngorongoro Crater and larger than many of Kenya's national parks. It is a massive playground for adventure and can be explored by horse, camel, vehicle, quad bike, helicopter and even hot-air balloon. I was there for one of the inaugural balloon flights and joined the local warriors early one morning to witness the balloon drifting above the cliffs of Loisaba. Rafting the Ewaso Ngiro and Engare Narok rivers on inflatable canoes is also popular at certain times of the year.

For wildlife densities Laikipia is second only to the Masai Mara, with Kenya's greatest concentrations of endangered animals, including more than half of the country's rhino and increasing numbers of wild dog. What makes it more remarkable is that the area is surrounded by community land and local farmers still wander the savanna with only their spears for protection.

STARBEDS

Loisaba's Kiboko Starbeds, established in 1998, has been dubbed 'the biggest bedroom in the world'. It consists of three sleeping platforms, which are raised high off the ground on stilts and have a partially covered thatched room. Guests sleep under the stars in specially designed beds called Mukokoteni, which are on wheels and can be rolled under cover, like a rickshaw, if the weather turns. It is a glorious experience and is hosted entirely by Samburu and Laikipiak Masai warriors. Starbeds has proved so successful that a second one, called Koija, has been built on the banks of the Ewaso Ngiro River and is a partnership with the Laikipiak Masai from the Koija community.

Another innovation here benefiting the community is Quad Bikes for Classrooms. There are eight all-terrain vehicles that can be hired out by the hour for bush breakfasts or game drives, and a large portion of this money goes into buying material to build classrooms. The Loisaba Community Trust (LCT) provides schooling for hundreds of children, as well as 26 scholarships for secondary school, three for college/university and two for trade school. And a visit to the local Masai village is made all the more poignant when you recognise that many are guides working at the lodge and that their children benefit in real ways from its profits.

Loisaba is not just about having fun. Whether you are on a quad bike, or staying at Starbeds, or buying a beaded belt from the craft group, you are always part of a much larger community initiative.

Semliki Safari Lodge & Apoka Safari Lodge & Sabyinyo Silverback Lodge

UGANDA, RWANDA

Semliki Safari Lodge

Semliki Wildlife Reserve

UGANDA

Nature is never far from the tents at Semliki (opposite). Monkeys can often be seen in the trees, leopard walk on the path right outside (below left) and kingfishers (below right) hunt near the river. The lodge has Lake Albert (above) – one of the East African Great Lakes – at its border.

Jonathan Wright, a Ugandan by birth, returned to his homeland in the mid-1990s determined to restore some of the wildlife areas that he knew from his childhood. He was shown a number of concessions in the well-known reserves, such as Queen Elizabeth Park and Murchison Falls, but he chose Semliki because it was remote, undeveloped and fascinating by its very nature. Proclaimed in 1932 as Toro Game Reserve, Semliki was the first game reserve in Uganda and was home to black-maned lion and the highest concentration of kob in the country.

'Two decades of civil war had taken its toll and poaching had reduced the numbers [of kob] from 30 000 to just a few hundred,' recalls Jonathan. 'There was nothing in the way of tourism development and we put in the game trails, built bridges, cut kilometres of roads and started to catalogue the bewildering array of species. The lodge was built out of local stone from a dilapidated building in the park and all the other structures were from local materials.'

Semliki's eight guest rooms are a mix of stone and golden canvas. Four overlook the forest and the distant blue mountains of the Congo and four look onto savanna plains towards the escarpment. I have been here twice in recent years and it is heartwarming to see how the wildlife

Semliki is in the Great Rift Valley and the escarpment looms high above the lodge (above). Getting active chimp trekking (below) through the Ugandan forests. Delicious meals are served in the gardens (right).

has recovered since the lodge was established and game patrols began. Kob now number 10 000 plus and the proud-looking territorial males are dotted all over the grasslands, which makes finding them easy. Much of the park vegetation is very dense (you could almost call it jungle) and the animals are wary of people, but this makes it all the more challenging and exciting.

Mark Vibbert, who runs the lodge with his wife Kristen, knows these animals well and one afternoon we positioned ourselves on an elephant trail to try our luck. Eventually a breeding herd appeared and mock-charged before retreating into the bush. What made the sighting very unusual was that these were a mix of savanna and forest elephant. The forest elephant are generally shorter with smaller, downward-pointing tusks.

Shoebill-spotting proved surprisingly easy by contrast. We glided over Lake Albert at dawn and watched fishermen pulling in their nets, dwarfed by the imposing massif of the Rwenzoris, which rose, snow capped, in the distance. Our guide picked out two or three shoebills fishing in the reed beds and I was delighted that we managed to approach within 10 metres of these astounding-looking birds with their large, boot-shaped beaks.

The University of Indiana has conducted chimp research here and noted that the primates often feed in the open savanna in a bipedal fashion, fuelling speculation that they could reveal important clues about humans. I took a walk through the thick forests with members of the Uganda Wildlife Authority and we heard the chimps calling through the forest.

'Where else do you get lion and chimpanzee living together, three types of pig, waterfalls that drop from the escarpment and both forest and savanna elephant?' Jonathan asked me. 'We've been here more than 10 years and only seen the tip of it.'

The soft, creamy linens, voluminous mosquito netting, golden canvas and polished wooden floors of one of the elegant guest rooms.

Saving Semliki

Semliki covers 550 square kilometres in the Western Rift Valley escarpment – a geological rampart that extends from Lake Albert southwards to Zambia's Luangwa Valley. Declared an important conservation area by the World Conservation Union on account of its high biodiversity, Semliki is right in the middle of it, between the plunging escarpment and the rise of the Rwenzori Mountains. The riparian forest, savanna, acacia woodland, rainforest, wetland and hardwood forest are home to more than 450 bird species, earning it a place amongst the Important Bird Areas of Uganda. These include four different types of hornbill and also the mysterious shoebill, a mega-tick for birders. Other specials are the red river hog, giant hog, African golden cat, short-snouted crocodile, forest and savanna elephant and chimpanzee.

Semliki, the only lodge in the area, has won awards for its contribution to conservation. An exciting new initiative, the Wild Places Conservation Trust, has also been launched by Mark and Kristen Vibbert (managers here for the past few years) to support wildlife protection, conservation of natural resources and implement community development projects along the reserve's borders.

Kob (top left), colobus monkey (top right) and shoebill (above) are regularly spotted at Semliki. The small tusks of this elephant (below) are indicative of the forest species, but larger ears suggest the more common savanna species.

Apoka Safari Lodge

Kidepo Valley National Park

UGANDA

A herd of elephant (opposite) making their way across the golden plains of the Narus Valley, with the lodge and the jagged mountains of Sudan as a dramatic backdrop. The lodge's swimming pool (above left) has been hewn out of a granite kopje and provides welcome relief on hot days. A dramatic welcome to Apoka (above right)! The rooms have high thatched roofs, canvas sides and cool neutral interiors.

It would be hard to find a more spectacular or remote location for a game lodge than Apoka in the Kidepo Valley National Park. This fertile valley lies on the very fringe of East Africa in the Karamoja region of northeastern Uganda.

'When we heard of the concession we almost didn't do it because of the enormity of the challenge,' says owner Jonathan Wright. 'But we had been to Kidepo twice before and our passion for the place won out.'

It was easy for me to see why. Standing on the balcony of the lodge, I could see streams of elephant and buffalo following the fertile course of the Narus River as it snaked its way northwards to the Nile. Lion and cheetah were stalking game on the plains and in the distance the jagged mountains rose from the golden grassland like a barrier of purple spears.

'An enormous amount of planning went into this lodge,' says Jonathan. 'Everything except the thatch had to be brought in by road. We're a day's drive from Kampala and planning was critical.'

Apoka's 10 tents are on stilts, with views of the mountains beyond. The cream canvas and neutral interiors ensure the atmosphere is calm and the wild drama that is going on outside takes centre stage. Zebra, buffalo and waterbuck frequent the camp and there is also a resident bull elephant. A special feature of the rooms are the outdoor baths, which are drawn whilst guests are enjoying sundowners. The lodge also has a rock pool hewn in the side of the granite kopje – it is the sort that makes you feel 10 years old again.

Pastoralists with no experience of tourism populate Karamoja. I can only imagine what they must have thought that evening when grilled lobster, which had been flown in that very day from Mombasa, appeared on the menu!

It is very easy to see game in large numbers on the open plains at Kidepo. On our game drives we saw lion, buffalo, elephant and giraffe amongst large numbers of other game, but for me it was the wilderness atmosphere and the walking that was even more remarkable. Climbing onto a high kopje one afternoon and gazing out over the plains I had the wonderful feeling of knowing that our group were probably the only tourists for hundreds of kilometres. And that is something.

The exterior baths (above) are drawn whilst guests enjoy sundowners. The romantic, hurricane-lamplit scene and the welcoming interiors of the rooms are a wonderful way to round off a day that is usually spent viewing the area's magnificent wilderness scenery and ample numbers and variety of animals, including patas monkey (top left).

The Landscape

Kidepo's savanna is interspersed with sausage trees and borassus palms and broken granite kopjes. And rising up from the valleys are steep mountains, with Mount Morungole on the park's southeastern boundary being the highest at 2 750 metres. The park is much drier than the rest of Uganda and has 86 mammal species, including 28 that are found nowhere else in the country. Amongst the more unusual species are Jackson's hartebeest and bohor reedbuck, as well as the tantalus and patas monkey. There are some 475 bird species here, including some big ticks such as the Karamoja apalis, Jackson's hornbill and black-breasted barbet. Cheetah are also commonly sighted and so are lion, which have a habit here of climbing sausage trees and kopjes to get a better view of the plains below.

Buffalo, waterbuck, zebra (top and right) and other game regularly graze in front of the lodge. Until the lodge was built, the Karamajong warriors (above right) were mainly herders, but they are now actively involved in the running of Apoka and also cook and provide entertainment for the guests.

SABYINYO SILVERBACK LODGE

Volcanoes National Park

RWANDA

Governors' Camps opened Sabyinyo Silverback Lodge in Rwanda's Volcanoes National Park in 2007. The lodge is situated at 2 350 metres on the edge of the Volcanoes National Park, just below the bamboo forests, with gorilla in very close proximity. Sabyinyo takes its name from one of the peaks of the volcanoes that rise up behind the lodge and it also has views of Muhabura, Gahinga, Karasimbi, Nkeno and Bisoke. It was here that primatologist Dian Fossey worked for 18 years (her story is told in *Gorillas in the Mist*) and, as she testified, these are mountains where 'you shiver more than you sweat'.

Sabyinyo is a cosy place with red-tiled roofs and ochre walls and has fires in every bedroom, as well as large and modern bathrooms – a welcoming thought when you return from your trek.

There are trips to see golden monkey and the surrounding lakes, but most people plan to see the gorillas. A maximum of 56 privileged people (no more than eight per group) get to see the seven habituated gorilla families each day. Our guide was Francois (he was one of Dian Fossey's trackers) and we followed him in single file up the slopes of Sabyinyo, keeping an eye out for the buffalo and elephant that also live here. At last, we came across the Hirwa Group relaxing amongst the thick bamboo. The silverback was three times my size, and despite the close proximity to his family of five females and five babies, he regarded us with gentle eyes. The time spent with these gentle primates was amazing and when our group, who had all previously been strangers, walked back towards the lodge, it was as if we all shared a very special secret.

There are only about 780 wild mountain gorilla on earth and they are all found in the Virungas, a chain of mountains that rise up between Rwanda, Uganda and the Democratic Republic of Congo. Of these, about 380 are found in the high mountains of Rwanda, alongside this warm and luxurious lodge.

Contact Details

CLASSIC SAFARI CAMPS OF AFRICA

P O Box 131357
Northmead 1511
Gauteng
South Africa
Tel: +27 (0)11 425-6413
Fax: +27 (0)11 425-6799
E-mail: classics@classicsafaricamps.com
Website: www.classicsafaricamps.com

SOUTH AFRICA

Ant's Nest and Ant's Hill Private Bush Homes
Waterberg, South Africa
Tel: +27 (0)14 755-3584/755-4296
E-mail: reservations@waterberg.net
Website: www.waterberg.net

Garonga Safari Camp
Makalali Conservancy
Tel: +27 (0)82 440-3522
E-mail: safari@garonga.com
Website: www.garonga.com

Jaci's Safari Lodge & Jaci's Tree Lodge
Madikwe Game Reserve
Tel: +27 (0)83 700-2071
E-mail: jaci@madikwe.com
Website: www.madikwe.com

NAMIBIA

Wolwedans Collection
NamibRand Nature Reserve
Tel: +264 (0)61 23-0616
E-mail: info@wolwedans.com.na and/or
reservations@wolwedans.com.na
Website: www.wolwedans.com

Mowani Mountain Camp
Twyfelfontein, Damaraland
Tel: +264 (0)61 23-2009
E-mail: mowani@visionsofafrica.com.na
Website: www.mowani.com

Onguma Safari Camps
Etosha National Park
Tel: +264 (0)61 23-2009
E-mail: onguma@visionsofafrica.com.na
Website: www.onguma.com

BOTSWANA

Selinda Camp
The Selinda Reserve
Tel: +267 625-0505
E-mail: reservations@selindareserve.com
Website: www.selindareserve.com

ZIMBABWE

The Hide
Hwange National Park
Tel: +263 (0)4 498-835/6
E-mail: info@thehide.com
Website: www.thehide.com

Musango Safari Camp
Lake Kariba/Matusadona National Park
Tel: +263 13 43358 or +263 61 3241/2
E-mail: steve@saflodge.co.zw or musango@mweb.co.zw
or steve@musango.com
Website: www.musango.com

Nduna Safari Lodge
Malilangwe
Tel: +263 (91) 225-7392/3/4
E-mail: reservations@malilangwe.org
Website: www.ndunasafarilodge.com

ZAMBIA

Tongabezi and Sindabezi
Victoria Falls
Tel: +26021 332 7468
E-mail: reservations@tongabezi.com
Website: www.tongabezi.com

Chongwe River Camp
Lower Zambezi National Park
Tel: +260 (0)1 286-808
E-mail: info@chongwe.com
Website: www.chongwe.com

Robin Pope Safaris
South Luangwa
Tel: +260 216 246090/1/2
E-mail: info@robinpopesafaris.net
Website: www.robinpopesafaris.net

MOZAMBIQUE

Benguerra Lodge
Bazaruto Archipelago
Tel: +27 (0)11 452-0641
E-mail: reservations@benguerra.co.za
Website: www.benguerra.co.za

TANZANIA

Greystoke Mahale
Mahale Mountains National Park
Tel: +255 (0)27 255-3819/20
E-mail: info@nomad.co.tz
Website: www.nomad-tanzania.com

Sand Rivers Selous
Selous Game Reserve
Tel: +255 (0)27 255-3819/20
E-mail: info@nomad.co.tz
Website: www.nomad-tanzania.com

KENYA

Tortilis Camp
Amboseli National Park
Tel: +254 (020) 604053 or 604054 or 603091
E-mail: info@chelipeacock.co.ke
Website: www.tortilis.com or www.chelipeacock.co.ke

Elsa's Kopje
Meru National Park
Tel: +254 (020) 604053 or 604054 or 603091
E-mail: info@chelipeacock.co.ke
Website: www.elsaskopje.com or www.chelipeacock.co.ke

Joy's Camp
Shaba National Reserve
Tel: +254 (020) 604053 or 604054 or 603091
E-mail: info@chelipeacock.co.ke
Website: www.joyscamp.com or www.chelipeacock.co.ke

Governors' Camp Collection – Governors' Camp, Little Governors' Camp, Il Moran Camp, Governors' Private Camp
Masai Mara
Tel: +254 (0)20 273-4000/5
E-mail: reservations@governorscamp.com
Website: www.governorscamp.com

Loldia House
Lake Naivasha
Tel: +254 (0)20 273-4000/5
E-mail: reservations@governorscamp.com
Website: www.governorscamp.com

Mfangano Island Camp
Lake Victoria
Tel: +254 (0)20 273-4000/5
E-mail: reservations@governorscamp.com
Website: www.governorscamp.com

Cottars 1920s Safari Camp
Masai Mara
Tel: +254 (0)73 377-3377 or 88-3681/96/8
E-mail: info@cottarsafaris.com or info@chelipeacock.co.ke
Website: www.cottars.com

Loisaba
Laikipia Plateau
Tel: +254 (0)62 31-072
E-mail: enquiries@loisaba.com or info@chelipeacock.co.ke
Website: www.loisaba.com

UGANDA, RWANDA

Semliki Safari Lodge
Semliki Wildlife Reserve
Tel: +256 (0)414 25-1182 or +256 772 489 497
E-mail: info@wildplacesafrica.com
Website: www.wildplacesafrica.com

Apoka Safari Lodge
Kidepo Valley National Park
Tel: +256 (0)414 25-1182 or +256 772 489 497
E-mail: info@wildplacesafrica.com
Website: www.wildplacesafrica.com

Sabyinyo Silverback Lodge
Volcanoes National Park
Tel: +254 (0)20 273-4000/5
E-mail: reservations@governorscamp.com
Website: www.governorscamp.com

First published in 2008 by Hornbill Press
15 Tokai Close, Marina da Gama
Muizenberg, Cape Town, 7945
South Africa

2 4 6 8 10 9 7 5 3 1

Publisher David Rogers
Project manager and editor Joy Clack
Designer Pete Bosman
Photographer and writer David Rogers
Illustrator Adam Carnegie
Proofreader Tessa Kennedy

Reproduction by Resolution Colour, Cape Town
Printed and bound by Craft Print International
Pte Ltd, Singapore

ISBN 978-0-620-39380-5 (Softcover)
ISBN 978-0-620-40411-2 (Hardcover)

PHOTOGRAPHIC CREDITS

Dana Allen: p 86 (bottom right); Ant's Nest: pp 16 (middle), 17 (bottom right), 18 (bottom left), 19 (top left); Daryl Balfour/Afripics.com: pp 106–107, 124 (top); Daryl Balfour/Gallo/Afripics.com: p 108; Herbert Brauer: 41 (top left); Hentie Burger: pp 43 (bottom left), 47 (bottom right); Steve Cunliffe: p 146 (below); Davison family: 61 (middle left); Johan du Plessis/Apoka Safari Lodge: pp 145 (above), 147 (above); Zara Fisher/Apoka Safari Lodge: p 146 (middle right); Emily Haynes: p 86 (middle); Paul Joynson-Hicks: pp 98 (bottom right), 101 (bottom right), 102 (bottom left & bottom middle), 103, 104–105 (top), 104 (bottom), 105 (middle left, middle right & bottom left); Beverly Joubert: pp 53 (top), 55 (middle right & bottom right); Rebke Klokke/Apoka Safari Lodge: pp 145 (above right), 146 (middle left), 147 (bottom left); Jacques Meyer: p 94 (top middle); Photo Paparazzi/Apoka Safari Lodge: pp 146 (above right), 147 (middle right); Gottfried Poennighaus: p 40; Robin Pope Safaris: pp 82 (top right); Selinda: p 53 (middle); Barry Wolhuter: pp 58 (top left), 60 (bottom left), 61 (middle right); Kim Wolhuter: p 67 (top left); Elsa Young: p 46 (top right).